SEE
JANE
LEAD

SEE
JANE
LEAD

99 Ways for Women to
Take Charge at Work

Lois P. Frankel, PhD

WARNER
BUSINESS
BOOKS™

NEW YORK   BOSTON

Warner Business Books
Hachette Book Group USA
237 Park Avenue
New York, NY 10169
Visit our Web site at www.HachetteBookGroupUSA.com

Warner Business Books is an imprint of Warner Books.
Warner Business Books is a trademark of Time Warner Inc. or an affiliated
company. Used under license by Hachette Book Group USA, which is not
affiliated with Time Warner Inc.

Book design by Fearn Cutler de Vicq

Printed in the United States of America

FIRST EDITION: APRIL 2007

10 9 8 7 6 5 4 3 2 1

Library of Congress Cataloging-in-Publication Data
Frankel, Lois P.
See Jane lead : 99 ways for women to take charge at work
    p. cm.
Includes bibliographical references and index.
ISBN-13: 978-0-446-57968-1 (alk. paper)
ISBN-10: 0-446-57968-8 (alk. paper)
1. Women executives. 2. Leadership in women. I. Title.
HD6054.3.F587 2006
658.4'092082—dc22
2006024639

This book is dedicated to the women of
MOSTE: Motivating Our Students Through Experience.
For twenty years you've donated your time, wisdom, and hearts to
at-risk girls by encouraging them to stay in school,
graduate, and go on to college.
Your commitment ensures we will have a next generation
of *diverse* women leaders. I honor *your* leadership by
donating a portion of the proceeds from this book to
MOSTE's Bernadine Robinson and
Jacqueline Miller Scholarship Funds.

Acknowledgments

The help, support, and guidance of many people went into writing this book. Thanking each of you seems hardly sufficient to express the depth of my gratitude, so I hope you know just how truly grateful I am for the gifts you have brought to me and, in turn, to the reader.

Diana Baroni, vice president and executive director at Warner Books—your confidence allows me to write in my own voice about the things that are so important to me, yet you challenge me to be better each time.

Chris Dao, former assistant director of publicity at Warner Books—your expertise helped me to go places I had only dreamed about before.

The entire team at Warner Books—there are far too many of you to mention without risking leaving someone out, but each of you is clearly superb at what you do, and the results prove it.

Bob Silverstein—what can I say? As a literary agent you're peerless, as a friend you're divine.

The women who took time from their busy lives as leaders to speak with me—please know that your insights, eloquence, and courage are what give this book heart.

Dr. Pam Erhardt, Dr. Kim Finger, Jessica Vaughn, and the team at Corporate Coaching International and Drloisfrankel.com—the way you intuitively alternate between leadership and followership, especially during some very rough days, is a gift I could not live without.

Kathleen Booth, director of organizational effectiveness at Warner Bros.—your generosity of spirit and time are given with such grace and are gratefully received.

My literary colleagues who took the time to speak with me and gave me permission to quote or reprint your work—I hope one day to be able to repay your kindness.

Contents

Introduction

My last two books focused on the myriad mistakes women make because they suffer from "nice girl syndrome." How I wish I was paid one dollar for each time an interviewer asked me, "Are you saying you have to be mean and nasty to achieve your goals?" One more time—and unequivocally—I say *No!* Nice girls are those who, in adulthood, continue to exhibit the behaviors they were taught in childhood that were appropriate for *little girls*. You know you have the syndrome when you take better care of everyone else than you do yourself, when you're afraid to take action for fear of disappointing or displeasing others, and when, despite the fact that you're a grown woman, you continue to act in accordance with the rules you were taught in childhood for how little girls were *supposed* to behave. In short, nice girls often suffer from "the disease to please."

Between *Nice Girls Don't Get the Corner Office* and *Nice Girls Don't Get Rich,* I've suggested 176 mistakes women make when pursuing their professional and financial goals. By now we've focused enough on errors, so this book doesn't focus on mistakes—only on strategies for unleashing your leadership capabilities in a variety of situations. It's not that we don't make mistakes related to leadership, because we do. Put a nice girl in a group of men and women, and she'll wait for a man—or a more powerful woman—to take the lead every time. Ask a nice girl to make a decision for the group and she'll take a poll before taking action. Give a nice girl a group of people to lead and she'll treat them like a family rather than a team looking to her for decisive, but humane, leadership. And in so doing she denies the talents she possesses that could serve to make her an exemplary leader. Women lead all the time—they just don't call it leadership.

Work and life experiences have enabled us to develop outstanding skills in balancing vision with strategy, taking risks, influencing others, motivating people to achieve their best, building teams of high performers, and capitalizing on our emotional intelligence—all essential ingredients for leading today's workers. In nontheoretical terms and using examples you can relate to, this book shows you the many ways in which you have already exhibited these and other leadership qualities. I wrote this book because I want you to see that you *are* a leader and you *do* have what it takes to lead a family, a project, a team, a department, a company, or a country. Who you choose to lead is up to you. This book provides you with the models to do it more confidently.

I often do an exercise in leadership classes and keynote addresses in which I ask the group to name the leaders they most admire. As you might imagine, they come up with a long list of men and a shorter list of women. On every list, though, Mother Teresa appears. *Of course.* She represents the stereotype of a female leader—passionate, compassionate, self-sacrificing, and service-oriented. There is no female equivalent of John F. Kennedy, Colin Powell, Jack Welch—or, thank goodness, Adolf Hitler, Jim Jones, or others of their ilk. What these men have in common is the ability to lead others toward predetermined goals—even goals that are, at times, not in the best interests of others. When someone, usually a woman, dares to mention Hillary Rodham Clinton, Condoleezza Rice, or Carly Fiorina, it sparks debate. Despite the fact that all of these women possess exemplary leadership capabilities, they aren't generally acknowledged and accepted as leaders. Why? In part because a woman's credibility doesn't follow her from successful achievement to successful achievement. She must prove herself with every challenge. As author Margaret Atwood said, "We still think of a powerful man as a leader and a powerful woman as an anomaly."

Too many women, perhaps you included, hesitate to step into the role of leadership for fear of being called too bossy, aggressive, egotistical—or worse yet, the dreaded B-word: *bitch*. For the same reasons we don't get the corner offices or riches we deserve, we don't lead in ways that will bring us to a new level of career or personal fulfillment through leadership. As a high school junior, I ran for class president against the young man I was dating at the time. When I won, the achievement had sufficiently damaged his ego to end to our relationship. When I ran against him again for senior-class president and won, it was as if I had personally assaulted his masculinity. Had the tables been turned, had he won one or both of those elections, I can't imagine it damaging the relationship to the same degree. It would have been socially acceptable.

Even in this day and age, women are socialized from birth to be first and foremost helpmates, not leaders. Ostracized by men *and* other women for being too "aggressive," and conflicted about engaging in any behavior that could be construed as less than collaborative, "nice girls" the world over simply don't lead. Put a woman in a room filled predominantly with men, and she will frequently acquiesce to their audibly louder voices, physically larger presence, and supposedly greater expertise. Ironically, if ever there was a time in history that cried out for women's leadership, that time is now. From boardrooms to nonprofit organizations to the military, there is a new generation of workers and volunteers who reject hierarchical leadership. A leader can no longer say "jump" and hear the response "how high?" And this is where you come in.

For centuries, women have unwittingly honed the quintessential qualities necessary for successful leadership. Whether acquired through nature or nurture, women's adeptness at building relationships, encouraging and motivating others to succeed, carefully crafting their communications, and creating environments of trust and safety represent but a few of the behaviors that qualify them as outstanding contemporary leaders. In considering the women whom I think portray the characteristics of effective leaders, I came up with this list:

- Hillary Rodham Clinton—former first lady of the United States and senator from New York.
- Anne Mulcahy—president of Xerox.
- Billie Jean King—pioneer in the field of women's tennis.
- Elizabeth Dole—senator from North Carolina.
- Pat Summitt—coach of the Tennessee Volunteers women's basketball team.
- Mary Kay Ash—founder of Mary Kay Cosmetics.
- Wilma Mankiller—former principal chief of the Cherokee Nation.
- Gail Evans—author and former executive with CNN.
- Debbi Fields—founder of Mrs. Fields Cookies.

- Coretta Scott King—civil rights leader.
- Mother Teresa—humanitarian.
- Sherry Lansing—former CEO of Paramount Pictures.
- Vera Wang—designer and head of a fashion empire.
- Margaret Thatcher—former prime minister of Great Britain.
- Golda Meir—former prime minister of Israel.
- Sandra Day O'Connor—former US Supreme Court justice.
- Meg Whitman—CEO of eBay.

You may wonder why I include certain women and not others. Despite the fact that she's successful and leads or has led various kinds of enterprises or causes, if a woman doesn't pass my "very scientific" beer test—*Would I enjoy sitting down and having a beer or cup of coffee with her?*—she didn't make the list. Great leaders are those who make others feel comfortable around them and possess high emotional intelligence. Without displaying an inordinate need to please others, they're just plain likable. If you're one of those people who say, "I'm not here to win a popularity contest, I'm here to get the job done," think again. People either won't follow or will sabotage the efforts of leaders they don't like.

There's one more thing each of the women included as role models have in common, and it defines leadership: *the ability to get people to follow them.* If there is a leader, there must be at least one follower, and what followers expect from leaders today are the behaviors and characteristics that women have traditionally been socialized to exhibit. Today's followers want to be muscled less and influenced more; criticized less and rewarded more; directed less and included more. It's not that men can't or don't display these qualities, but rather that women, when given the opportunity, tend to display them with greater ease, confidence, and comfort.

After creating the list of women leaders I most admire, I then created a matrix of the behaviors they were known for, and to even my surprise, I found that these women have several things in common:

- Clear vision of what they want to accomplish.
- Ability to balance the strategic with the tactical.
- Willingness to take risks.
- Ability to influence others.
- Ability to inspire and motivate others.
- Ability to build teams of people to help them achieve their vision.
- High emotional intelligence.

I say it was a surprise because I had already created a list of behaviors I thought were essential ingredients to leadership success, and each of the above behaviors was *already* on my list!

The exercise not only served to reinforce that I was on the right track but also formed the basis of each chapter in this book. Beginning with development of your vision straight through to the methods for achieving that vision through planning and people, *See Jane Lead* provides a blueprint for how you can lead in nearly any situation. Are there other behaviors that are required for strong leadership? Yes—and there are plenty of other books that write about them. My desire was to write a book that focuses on women's *natural* strengths, because these form the foundation of our success.

Each chapter details why I believe the leadership behaviors listed above are inherent to the repertoire of skills possessed by most women, ways in which you've probably exhibited these behaviors in your day-to-day life, and how you can hone the behaviors by following the models and coaching tips provided throughout and at the end of each chapter. I include the stories of women leaders, some of them universally known but most of them everyday women known primarily in their own fields. Unlike other books, however, this one is not about *their* stories—it's about *you*. I use my interviews with these women leaders only as a means of providing you with ideas for how you can engage in the same behaviors that made them successful as well as learn from their mistakes.

As an executive coach, I've seen both men and women make mistakes that cause others to doubt their leadership potential. Leadership mistakes are not the exclusive domain of women. But I believe that our families, our communities, and our countries suffer when capable women exhibit a reluctance to lead. I'm often asked if I think women make *better* leaders than men. No, I don't think that. Leaders aren't good because they belong to one gender or the other, they're good because *they possess the qualities and characteristics needed for a particular time and place*. It's been said that great leaders aren't interchangeable. Patton was a great leader during World War II, but I don't think he could effectively lead today's troops. Similarly, whereas Mary Kay Ash, founder of Mary Kay Cosmetics, built a great company at a time when women wanted opportunities to be financially independent and spend time with their families, I don't think she could have replaced Carly Fiorina at Hewlett-Packard. No, gender is not a prerequisite for leadership.

The essence of good leadership is the ability to take people to places they *need* to go, not necessarily where they *want* to go. If you're a mother, you know the challenge of convincing a child to go to school on a day that she really doesn't want to be there.

Volunteer coordinators in nonprofit organizations are faced with the daunting task of motivating well-intentioned but unpaid staff to achieve organizational goals. During difficult financial times, supervisors and managers bear the burden of maintaining corporate financial stability in the face of layoffs, mergers, and acquisitions. Through each of these challenges runs the common thread of leading people where they *need* to go. At the heart of it, leadership requires a set of skills and behaviors that anyone can learn, but few choose to embrace. Leadership in the twenty-first century is different from leadership in the mid–twentieth century is different from leadership in the pre–twentieth century. What makes leadership different through the ages are the needs of followers.

Throughout this book, I use the term *followers*. It's not intended in a demeaning or disparaging way, but rather as a means of creating a visual picture of you as a leader and people aligning behind you and your agenda. Just as Mary Kay, Golda Meir, Carly Fiorina, and Billie Jean King got people to follow them, you need people to follow you if you want to lead. Today's followers are similar to the followers of past centuries in that they want strong leaders. The difference is that they also want to participate in the decision-making process, want to be recognized for their accomplishments, and want autonomy in how they achieve organizational goals. Who better fills these requirements than women? We have never had the luxury of being able to lead through intimidation. Ask a mother where that gets you. We haven't been able to lead through brute force. Any woman can tell you what kinds of names that will get you called. Women have traditionally had to lead through their wits, influence, and motivational abilities. And the time for putting these and other uniquely feminine leadership traits to good use has finally arrived.

If you're reading this book, I already know something about you. You want to lead, not for the sake of power or control, but to make a difference. You want to harness the energies of those around you for the benefit of everyone associated with the agenda you are trying to achieve. You want to reach the goals associated with your business or organization because in doing so you will serve a greater good. And you want to achieve your full potential. In this book, I tell you how to do just that. Not only have I led projects large and small, but I have helped countless people tap into their own leadership abilities as well. I have studied leaders and leadership from a broad perspective. I am not so egotistical as to say the ideas contained in this book are uniquely mine. They are the culmination of a lifetime of leading, reading, following, and teaching about leadership. Wherever appropriate and possible, I give credit to those from whom I've learned.

As with all of my books, you'll find a self-assessment in the first chapter that will help you identify your strengths and areas for development—this time related to leadership behaviors. Each category in the inventory correlates to a subsequent chapter on the same topic; once you know your score, you can go immediately to those chapters that will give you the most help, or go first to those that will reinforce your existing strengths. Because I believe each of us must lead with our strengths, I focus specifically on those leadership behaviors in which women already excel—even if they don't realize it. From balancing strategy and tactics to building a team, women have had business and life experiences that bolster their leadership capabilities. The purpose of this book is to illuminate those for you, help you build on them, and give you models to maximize your leadership performance using them.

If you want to be a great leader, then approach it as a skill to be learned, just as you learned the skills that brought you to where you are today. My hope is that reading this book will be another step on your leadership journey, for leading is just that—a journey, not a destination. You'll never become a great leader by reading just one book, but one book can put you on the path to great leadership.

SEE
JANE
LEAD

CHAPTER ONE

The Feminization of Leadership

The day will come when man will recognize woman as his peer, not only at the fireside, but in councils of the nation. Then, and not until then, will there be the perfect comradeship, the ideal union between the sexes that shall result in the highest development of the race.

—Susan B. Anthony

People often ask me how I choose the subject matter for my books. I tell them it always comes from having such a burning desire to share something with others that if I didn't, I would feel my life's mission was not complete. That's precisely why I wrote *this* book. I believe we live in a time when women's leadership and influence aren't just needed—they're required. More important, I *know* that women have the capability, strength, courage, and heart to lead communities, businesses, nonprofit organizations, and grassroots groups to places they need to go. They've done it for centuries. You may not think you have much in common with Avon's president Andrea Jung or former director of the Red Cross Elizabeth Dole, but this book will help you to see that you do—and that if ever there was a time your leadership was needed, the time is now.

You also may not aspire to be a CEO, vice president, or director of an organization, but chances are you find yourself in a position where you want to influence others. That's leadership. You may be responsible for a small committee of the PTA. That's leadership. Or you might have ideas that contribute to creating change in an organization of which you are a member. That's leadership, too. Women lead all the time—they just don't call it leadership. They think of it as working toward a common goal, achieving results through people, or simply doing what needs to be done. In fact, that's what leadership is all about.

A woman's way of leading hasn't always been valued, but there's a change occurring in society that people are hesitant to talk about. It's what I call the *feminization of leadership*. To discuss it openly would mean challenging how we have traditionally looked at leadership—and *followership*. It would also require embracing a concept that many people find threatening: Command-and-control, top-down leadership no longer works. When someone in authority says "jump," employees, children, and volunteers no longer reply "how high?" The truth is, what followers expect from leaders in the first decade of the twenty-first century—and perhaps beyond—are the behaviors and characteristics that women have traditionally been socialized to exhibit. Throughout history, with little or no formal authority, women have influenced direction, change, and outcomes—they were simply never so bold as to call it leadership!

It doesn't mean that men can't or don't display these qualities, but rather that women tend to do so with greater ease, confidence, and comfort—so long as it's not called the L-word, *leadership*. The changing face of leadership is threatening to men because it requires thinking about the subject in a way that is counter to their own socialization and, in some cases, education. Similarly, women may feel threatened because it asks them to assume responsibility in ways they may never have before and to call attention to skills they have been admonished to hide.

"Nice girls" have a particularly difficult time assuming leadership roles and doing it effectively. When they do, they often try to make everyone happy (which, as you know, is impossible), delay decision making by trying to get *everyone's* buy-in, hesitate to take necessary risks for fear of offending the powers that be, and communicate in ways that undermine their confidence and credibility. Ironically, each of these behaviors could work to the advantage of women—if only they would balance them with new behaviors that contribute to more effective leadership. In other words, stepping fully away from the nice-girl messages learned in childhood, and into adulthood, is all it would take for a woman to be a phenomenal leader for this age. Of course, that's one giant step.

Society has done both men and women a disservice by placing the onus of leadership responsibility squarely on the shoulders of men. It makes men reluctant to admit when they feel incapable of or ineffectual at leadership and women reluctant to openly suggest that they might be able to do a better job of it. Nonetheless, we are at a turning point where both genders will have to become more comfortable with assuming roles they have traditionally rejected. This turning point is caused by evolving worker attitudes and values that women are best suited to address. Just as women have, in the past, had to learn from men how to manage using styles that did not come naturally to them, men will now have to learn from women the ways of bringing out the best in today's workforce.

Despite the fact that American productivity continues to decline, most major corporations continue to be led almost exclusively by white males. A recent study conducted by Catalyst, this country's premier women's research group, reports that although women make up 46.4 percent of the labor force, only seven *Fortune* 500 CEOs are women. Women constitute only 5.2 percent of the top earners and hold only 7.9 percent of the highest titles in these companies.

THE CATALYST PYRAMID:
US WOMEN IN BUSINESS

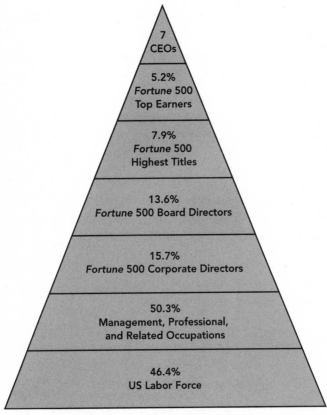

7
CEOs

5.2%
Fortune 500
Top Earners

7.9%
Fortune 500
Highest Titles

13.6%
Fortune 500 Board Directors

15.7%
Fortune 500 Corporate Directors

50.3%
Management, Professional,
and Related Occupations

46.4%
US Labor Force

Sources: Current Population Survey, Annual Averages 2004
Catalyst, *2003 Catalyst Census of Women Board Directors*
Catalyst, *2002 Catalyst Census of Women Corporate Officers and Top Earners*

Turning to politics, as of January 2006 only 15 percent of all elected representatives to the US Congress were women. Of those women, 24 percent are women of color, but they all serve in the House of Representatives with *no women of color* serving in the Senate. This is fairly consistent with the average of 16 percent of women holding seats in parliaments around the world. Out of 180 countries, only 11 have women heads of state. What's missing at the top is not just a *female* perspective, but a broad diversity of opinions and skills.

Paradoxically, when those who possess power and control are threatened by circumstance, they are inclined to hold even tighter to their authority. When status quo is thus maintained, organizations and societies lose. With diversity, however, comes the promise of positive change, as shown by another Catalyst study. This one that found companies with the most women in senior management positions had a *35 percent higher return on equity* and a *34 percent higher total return to shareholders.* Similarly, the law firm Dickstein Shapiro reports that in 1994 when it had 63 women attorneys out of 213, profit per partner was $364,000 annually. In 2004, when the number of women had grown to 122 out of 363 attorneys, the per-partner profit had increased to $815,000. Linda Kornfeld and Robin Cohen, attorneys with Dickstein Shapiro, say they believe women leaders are making great contributions for the following reasons:

- Women executives are more likely to consult with others—experts, employees, and fellow business owners—when developing strategies.
- Women executives have a greater natural tendency to deal comfortably with multitasking.
- Women executives have fewer competitive tendencies and often seek a more collaborative approach.

- Women executives tend to focus on the big picture when making important business decisions or developing strategies.
- Women executives stress relationship building as well as fact gathering.
- Women executives are more likely to talk through business approaches and incorporate the ideas of others before making final decisions.

These and other factors combine to make me conclude that women have not only the *ability* to become great leaders for our time but also the *responsibility* to do so. Just as women are entrusted with the primary responsibility for bearing and raising the next generation, they have a similar responsibility to ensure that the systems and institutions upon which the next generation will rely are strong and healthy. Women must cease colluding with those who either subconsciously or systematically deny them inclusion. Eleanor Roosevelt once said, "No one can make you feel inferior without your consent." When you allow others to do this, you *collude* with them to remain in an inferior position. Instead, women must come to understand how to maximize the use of their natural gifts within a system that tries to deny the value and necessity of these gifts. A formidable task, but none too difficult for a group that for centuries has relied on its wits and inner strength to triumph over discrimination and oppression.

WHY NICE GIRLS DON'T LEAD

Most workshops that I conduct include a module on collaborative problem solving. It's videotaped and played back so that participants can see themselves as others see them. The instructions, given in advance, ask participants to wait until the camera is on before they begin work on the problem. With only two exceptions in nearly twenty years, after the camera begins recording, the first person to speak has been a man. Regardless of seniority or expertise, women are reticent to take the lead. The reasons for this are as different as women themselves. When they do exhibit leader behaviors (particularly when they do so before being asked), they face a wide array of subtle and not-so-subtle reactions—from both men and women. Included among the reactions with which they are forced to contend:

- Being called names (usually behind their backs) that assault their femininity.
- Anger that is expressed blatantly or passive-aggressively.
- Having their ideas openly challenged, rather than built on.
- Having their ideas overlooked only to be repeated as original by men in the group.
- Being excluded from future meetings.
- Having information that enables them to make good judgments withheld.
- Challenges to their "right" to lead (i.e., "Who does she think she is?").
- Later being given more menial assignments that are designed to keep them in their place.
- Being placated.
- Being openly derided.

In the face of such negative reactions, it's no wonder that women are reluctant to lead! This is what makes it so important for women to consciously view these reactions as natural responses to a system trying to maintain status quo, and not to collude with them.

In the 1977 classic *Games Mother Never Taught You: Corporate Gamesmanship for Women,* Betty Lehan Harragan used masculine metaphors and definitions to help women better understand how to win the game of business. Although groundbreaking at the time, the book set the stage for women to assume that they inherently lacked knowledge or skills to compete on the corporate playing field. Subsequent books followed suit, and soon the very essence of the woman leader was lost in assertiveness training, tailored suits (with little bow ties for a time), and sports jargon. As a result, women chose to hide their natural abilities and instead attempted to emulate the higher-valued behaviors associated with the masculine style of leadership.

I was honored when Dr. Judy Rosener, professor emerita of the University of California–Irvine's Paul Merage School of Business, graciously agreed to speak with me about this. In 1990, Dr. Rosener wrote an article for the *Harvard Business Review* titled "Ways Women Lead." Although she's written many books and articles since, this piece represents the seminal thoughts on the topic of women and leadership. She was ahead of the curve then, and she still is. That article was the first to suggest that women possess a different style of leadership from men—but one that's equally effective. She shifted the thinking for many of us from *I have to be more like a man to succeed as a leader* to *The skills I bring to the workplace, whether developed by nature or nurture, have intrinsic value.* Judy wrote, "Women's success shows that a nontraditional leadership style is well-suited to the conditions of some work environments and can increase an organization's chances of surviving in an uncertain world."

When I had the chance to interview her sixteen years after the article's publication, I was anxious to get her thoughts about how things have changed in the intervening years. Here's what she shared with me:

> *The biggest difference today is that women no longer believe that to be a leader is to be a male. My article provided some "aha" moments for women, so that they now believe that in a fast-changing, highly technological, globalized environment there are certain attributes that are particularly effective that they happen to exhibit. Women are far more comfortable doing what they do naturally and less comfortable with being trained to be like men. That's why women are leaving corporations and starting their own businesses. Flexibility, collaboration, and multitasking are things women do well because of either socialization or nature. Women today have moved from a "fitting-in" model (to succeed they have to fit in) to an "organizational fit" model, which means* I'm going to join an organization where what I do is valued and rewarded. *It may be subconscious, but the women I talk to constantly are transitioning. They don't want to change to be successful. Women have to know and understand the environment in which they work but not think that their leadership skills present a problem, because they're not the problem.*

I agree wholeheartedly. In the past, women who did not want to sublimate their natural abilities were left with three options: (1) remain silent and in nonleadership positions; (2) leave corporate America to start their own businesses; or (3) leave business entirely—to parent, retire, teach, what have you. Although businesses are slowly (and somewhat reluctantly) beginning to embrace this notion of a different but equal leadership style, the result continues to be a migration of women leaders away from business at the very time when their skills are required to better understand how to improve productivity and morale. Option 2, starting their own businesses, is increasingly being exercised, with the number of women-owned companies growing at twice the rate of all businesses between 1997 and 2002. They contribute more than $2.8 trillion in revenues to the US economy and employ in excess of 9.2 million people.

Women can, and must, combine their socialization and natural instincts to provide the kind of leadership necessary to unleash a wider array of individual and team gifts than are present in today's workplace. It's simply a matter of harnessing their talents, reframing them in a way that they can be better showcased, and augmenting them with complementary behaviors to provide a well-rounded (and much-needed) approach to the business of leadership.

WHY WOMEN AND WHY NOW?

Leaders can be successful only insofar as they accurately and adequately respond to the immediate needs of their followers. In other words, *you must be a leader for your time*. It has been suggested that generals George S. Patton and Norman Schwarzkopf could not have been interchanged. The needs of the troops dramatically shifted during the forty-year interim between World War II and the Gulf War. Whereas Patton's command-and-control style would most likely have been received with resistance by Gulf War troops, Schwarzkopf's tendency to listen carefully to the suggestions and needs of others before making decisions might have been perceived as indecisive or soft by World War II soldiers.

On the business front, and technology aside, it is highly doubtful that in this day and age Tom Watson Sr. could successfully build the giant we know as IBM, or that Henry Ford could pioneer automobile manufacturing. Achieving their respective visions was possible only because they understood the needs of their followers *at the time*. Watson's full-employment policy was designed to appeal to the insecurities of workers during the Depression. He knew that allowing everyone to work (albeit on reduced schedules) rather than laying people off would secure their loyalty during more prosperous times. Henry Ford's automation of the manufacturing process provided a kind of financial stability within a hierarchical framework that workers of his day craved. Both men accurately read the employment climate and used it to their advantage. Similarly, I seriously doubt that Ronald Reagan could have been elected in place of FDR, or that Mary Kay Ash could have successfully started and marketed her product at the turn of the twentieth century. Both these leaders were successful in their quests only because they understood the social climate and needs of their followers *at the time*.

The same holds true in society today. Bringing out the best in people is a far different game than it was even ten years ago. The reasons for this shift in worker expectations are varied and complex. They include the effects of a decade of downsizing, technological advances, shifts in workforce demographics, changes in societal patterns such as increased numbers of divorces and single-parent families, and globalization. Combined, they create a scenario in which reliance on the traditional paradigms of command and control, management over leadership, and position power no longer work.

The Demise of Command-and-Control Leadership

The days of command-and-control leadership are long gone. This style was characterized by blind adherence to strict rules, a rigidly defined and top-down hierarchical chain of command, and an emphasis on winning at any cost. Workers would respond to management demands or directives simply because they believed that the people (usually men) in authority deserved to be respected. It was born out of a *masculine military model* that assumed that those who possessed no formal authority had no real purpose other than to carry out the directives of management.

Although command-and-control leadership was the preferred style for the better part of the last century, it has for the most part outlived its usefulness. Even in paramilitary organizations such as fire departments, police forces, and other emergency operations, command-and-control management is of limited use. The primary way in which it continues to be valuable is during times of extreme emergency. When it works, it provides a model by which everyone can operate with maximum efficiency. When it doesn't, however, you wind up with a situation similar to what we witnessed in the aftermath of Hurricane Katrina: confusion, lack of real leadership, an unclear chain of command, and finger pointing rather than problem solving. And when it does work, it works only for the moment. Command-and-control leadership does nothing to improve morale or productivity during nonemergency situations, which is an important issue that paramilitary organizations are being forced to examine more carefully when considering how to motivate their increasingly diverse workforces. The command-and-control model worked up until now for a number of reasons:

- The workforce, primarily white male, understood and respected the hierarchy.
- Manufacturing, the country's economic engine, lent itself to using the model.

- Years of war and the threat of war enabled men and women alike to easily comprehend the bounds of command and control.
- A relatively uneducated workforce allowed itself to be governed by the belief that those in authority knew best.
- Women and people of color were hesitant to challenge the model for fear of losing hard-won gains.

In this day of highly skilled and educated workers in which information technology, telecommuting, and flat organizations abound, command and control simply doesn't work. People don't want to be told what to do, when to do it, and how it should be done. Not only do they not want it, they won't allow it. Managers who continue to rely on the style (and there are many more of those around than you might expect) are met with *subversive compliance:* people doing exactly as they are told and finding nonverbal ways to sabotage the process. Consider the following examples:

- Jim, the manager of accounting, tells Jan, an accounting clerk, to prepare a report in a particular way. Jan tries to tell Jim that doing it this way doesn't take into consideration several key factors, but Jim's command-and-control style precludes him from listening. Jan dutifully prepares the report as she was told. When Jim makes a presentation to management, Jan knows full well that Jim won't be able to answer certain questions without the additional data that she suggested. Instead of discussing it again with Jim, Jan thinks, *If this is what you want, this is what you get,* and allows Jim to be ill-prepared and embarrassed in front of his management.

- Trey is a new PC salesperson at a local electronics store. During his training period, he politely suggests adding several services to ensure customer satisfaction that go beyond what the store currently provides. Kristen, his command-and-control manager, instructs him in no uncertain terms to do it her way or face possibly failing the store's probationary period. Several weeks later, when a customer asks for services that he had suggested but Kristen rejected, Trey refers him to a competitor he knows who does provide those services.

- Barbara is the manager of administration for a prestigious law firm. She has repeatedly tried to influence Bill, the firm's managing partner, to revise outdated policies related to compensation and benefits for the administrative staff. Command-and-control Bill refuses to budge, believing that working for the firm is privilege enough. When staff members apply for positions outside the firm, Barbara willingly gives glowing recommendations so that they can move on to more lucrative assignments, while the firm loses valuable talent.

As you can see, subversive compliance caused by outmoded command-and-control leadership approaches can cost organizations unnecessary expense in terms of turnover, mistakes, loss of customers or clients, and reduced productivity. The ways in which women have traditionally approached work and leadership provide a fresh new model from which managers of both sexes could learn and profit.

Management versus Leadership

The demise of command-and-control leadership has illuminated the differences between management and leadership. Of late, much has been written on the topic, but the difference is best summarized by a simple phrase: *You manage functions and lead people.* For example, you manage budgets, hiring processes, quantifiable outcomes, or information systems, but you can't manage people. The command-and-control style was an attempt to *manage* people, but as I've pointed out, it ultimately proved ineffective as workplace attitudes changed. People don't want to be *managed*—they want to be *led,* and they want to be led by caring, humane leaders. In this regard, *management* is more closely aligned with masculine leadership traits, whereas *leadership* is more in tune with a woman's strengths.

I believe women are ideally suited to do both—manage *and* lead. Why? Look at it this way: If you're able to schedule your hair appointment to coincide with picking up the family's dry cleaning but before you have to take the dog to the kennel so that you can leave on a business trip, then managing a schedule, budget, or project is no sweat. On the other hand, when you're responsible for getting the entire family on board with taking a trip to see your in-laws the same weekend that everyone wanted to watch the Super Bowl, then leading a reluctant staff in an organizational change effort becomes a breeze. From running households to PTA meetings and church fund-raisers, it's likely you've honed the skills needed to lead *and* manage.

The importance of differentiating leadership from management was brought home during an association conference presentation that I made several years ago. This was a group of people involved in various aspects of the hospitality industry—conference planners, travel agents, representatives of hotels, and so on. After one man disagreed with how I differentiated leadership and management, a woman who led the staff of housekeepers at a well-known hotel chain took issue with him. She agreed wholeheartedly that you can't manage people, and added that if anyone ever doubts it, just try to *manage* people whose sole function is to clean hotel rooms. There is nothing more straightforward or easier to measure than how the rooms are cleaned, but getting people to do it well is another story. Success in this field, she insisted, depends on leadership, not management.

Whether it's housekeepers, zookeepers, or barkeepers—you simply can't *manage* people. Trying to do so is a bit like teaching a pig to sing: You frustrate yourself and annoy the pig. The ways in which women, without formal control, authority, or title, have gained the support of followers by exhibiting leadership qualities, not management skills, hold the key to successful leadership in the new millennium.

A New Definition of Power and Leadership

During a presentation I was making to a group of health care providers on the topic of motivating today's workforce, I commented that the new generation of employees no longer "salutes" those in authority. A ripple of agreement in the form of heads vehemently nodding and polite laughter came from the back of the auditorium, where I could see a row of middle-aged men and women in uniform. I decided to enlist them in underscoring my contention. Pointing to the back row, I said, "It seems to me as if you would be in a good position to talk to us about employees saluting." These participants from the military willingly and poignantly described the shift that has taken place over the past two decades: Personnel no longer do as they are told simply because someone in a position of power tells them to. They also explained that this has caused difficulties with some longer-term senior staff who could not adjust to new and more appropriate styles of leadership.

In the workplace—and not only the military workplace—leaders have traditionally relied on what's called *position power*. This is the power and authority that typically accompanied titles such as *supervisor, manager, director,* and *vice president,* or *sergeant, lieutenant,* and *general*. Leaders relied on position power because inherent to it was the threat of punishment if their directives were not followed. "My way or the highway" typified reliance on this form of power. But new-generation workers no longer respect position power. They have seen political leaders with position power publicly debased because of personal peccadilloes, watched as those with position power unceremoniously terminated their company-loyal parents, and experienced firsthand a decline in respect for position power in the family. Position power doesn't motivate or faze them.

Since women have not been the primary beneficiaries of position power, they have not learned to rely on it. In fact, women are uncomfortable with even using the word *power* in relation to themselves. My interest in women and power was piqued in the late 1980s when I had a private psychotherapy practice working with career women. I would often comment to clients who held senior-level corporate positions that it seemed incongruent that one so powerful would allow herself to be treated in this way or that. The response was always some form of *Me? Powerful? I'm not powerful*. In my audiotape *Women and Power: Understanding Your Fear/Releasing Your Potential,* I explain the reasons for this:

- Social messages learned early in childhood imply that power diminishes femininity.
- Because men have traditionally wielded the power, for a

woman to think of herself as powerful means that she must take power away from important male figures in her life—father, brother, grandfather, teachers, or the like.

- Powerful women are often singled out and labeled with any number of pejoratives.
- Until recently, there has been a paucity of powerful female role models.

Since noticing the response of the women in my practice, I have begun each presentation that I make related to power in the workplace by singling out a woman and saying, "You look pretty powerful to me." With few exceptions, the woman shifts uncomfortably in her seat and mumbles something in denial. Next, I turn to a man in the audience and make the same comment. With even fewer exceptions, the response from the man is a comment or body language that in some way affirms my observation. The ensuing discussion of power and what it means clarifies the distinctions between male and female definitions of power. Whereas men often define being powerful as getting *someone else* to do what they want or having control over others, women tend to define it as getting to do what *they* want or having control over themselves.

It certainly isn't that women are not powerful, because they are. It's that women wield power *differently* from men and in a way that better meets the expectations of contemporary followers. By necessity, they have had to rely on an assortment of techniques to meet their needs and the needs of those who depend on them, which is why women possess a wider array of influence skills and exhibit less concern for position power or command-and-control leadership. Women's power is often derived from gaining allegiance and loyalty by understanding and addressing the needs of others. Women not only are socialized to do this better but in fact have had years of practice at it.

Similarly, a common theme ran through the interviews I conducted for this book. Nearly every woman, when asked what constitutes her leadership philosophy, included some mention of values-based leadership. Values formed the core of how women went about enacting everyday leadership behaviors. From developing a vision to creating a high-performing team and taking risks, women returned time and again to their values to determine the "rightness" of their direction. This reveals yet one more way in which the uniqueness of a woman's perspective forges a leadership model that is so critical for our time.

A WOMAN'S LEADERSHIP MODEL

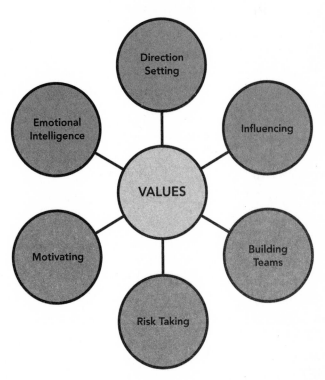

WHAT FOLLOWERS REALLY WANT FROM LEADERS

There is no shortage of books that describe the necessary qualities of successful leaders. From gurus like Warren Bennis, Peter Drucker, John Kotter, and Max De Pree, we consistently hear that successful leadership includes the ability to:

- Create a vision, align people behind it, and develop a plan for executing it.
- Communicate in a way that inspires trust and confidence.
- Motivate followers to sustain the effort required to meet organizational goals.
- Build teams that understand and value interdependence and synergy.
- Exhibit emotional intelligence.
- Take risks that will benefit the organization.
- Develop a strong network that will support goal attainment and professional success.

A close look at the list reveals that these behaviors are identical to the ones women routinely exhibit given their own socialization as nurturers, accommodators, and caretakers. It is precisely these factors that lead me to claim *leadership is a woman's art.* Women's survival has always depended on exhibiting the very behaviors desperately needed in society today. At the same time, most of the behaviors on the list have also been pejoratively referred to as "soft skills." Having nothing to do with command and control, they have traditionally been relegated to lower levels of importance and not perceived by many leaders to be critical success factors.

Whether it's bolstering the flagging confidence of a follower, teaching groups of people how to become teams, or simply building the kinds of relationships that mutually support both leader and follower, women eminently fit the bill. In tribal villages, families, PTAs, hospitals, schools—anyplace where taking care of the most basic, but often overlooked, needs of people is important—women are at the center of the activity. Whether by nature or nurture, women's focus has always been on ensuring the well-being of others, while concurrently being required to meet the goals inherent to their roles in the village, family, or workplace. The ability of women to understand the needs of their followers and create a means for moving organizations forward by attending to these needs cannot be underestimated. Further, women are not hampered by old paradigms that merely perpetuate the status quo. As relative newcomers to the boardroom, we possess precisely what is needed to shift from the tried, but no longer true, ways of doing things to fresh new approaches toward meeting business objectives.

One way in which I attempt to make the key concepts of leadership come alive for participants in my leadership workshops is to have them identify leaders from their own lives who brought out the best in them. I ask them to name the people who made a significant difference in their lives—teachers, parents, coaches, clergy, spouses, bosses, and friends—and then tell the group what made this person so effective. Regardless of the geographic location, the size of the organization, or the nature of the work performed by the participants, their lists nearly always include these same behaviors:

- Treated me as a human being, not just an employee.
- Believed in me even when I didn't believe in myself.

- Trusted me.
- Was interested in my well-being—not just what was best for the company.
- Went to bat for me.
- Kept his or her word.
- Stretched me by setting high expectations *and* giving me the tools to achieve them.
- Asked for my opinion—and listened to the answer.
- Set a good example.
- Was honest—would admit when he or she was wrong.
- Kept me well-informed.
- Didn't punish me for making mistakes, but gave me helpful feedback—both positive and negative.
- Showed enthusiasm for his or her work.
- Was firm but fair.

People report that when these characteristics are present, they exhibit uncommon commitment to the leader. Again, it's not about any particular technique or unusual skill, but rather about how people are treated by a leader and the degree to which the leader interacts with them first and foremost as human beings. Most of the items on the list are behaviors in which women engage naturally. Openly sharing information, encouraging, trusting, and so forth are all key components of the partnership style of power and interactive leadership style.

As difficult as it is for many women to acknowledge, leadership is not currently, and has never been, the exclusive domain of men. The ways women lead are different but no less valuable—as women have been led to believe. In an effort to maintain control and dominance, those who have traditionally held power have minimized our contributions; in turn, women have minimized their potential as leaders. Returning to the concept that *you must be a leader for your time*, I reiterate that *the time is now for women leaders*. If ever there was a need to bring out the best in people, create interdependent work groups, and inspire people to overcome the mediocrity that plagues products and services, that time is now—and women hold the key for doing it successfully, compassionately, and capably.

WOMEN AND LEADERSHIP SELF-ASSESSMENT

An essential ingredient of leadership success is the capacity to assess your own strengths and areas that need development—and make changes to your course when called for. Doing this allows you to model the way for your followers to do the same. Women are particularly good at this—it's why they read "Dear Abby," listen to Dr. Laura, and buy the majority of self-help books on the market! Here's an opportunity to identify your leadership strengths and opportunities for growth. Completing the following inventory will also provide you with a road map for making good use of this book.

Answer each of the following questions using the scale provided. Don't overthink your answers—go with your first instinct. Be as honest as possible. Don't indicate what you think you *should* do; note what you *actually* do. If you aren't currently in a leadership position, think of situations in which you may have been called on or had the opportunity to exhibit the behavior described and what you did in those situations. Most important, be candid. It will do you no good to try to look good. Similarly, don't be overly critical of yourself. In either case, you'll only be fooling yourself.

4 = Is characteristic of me *nearly all the time*

3 = Is *usually* characteristic of me

2 = Is *sometimes* characteristic of me

1 = Is *rarely* characteristic of me

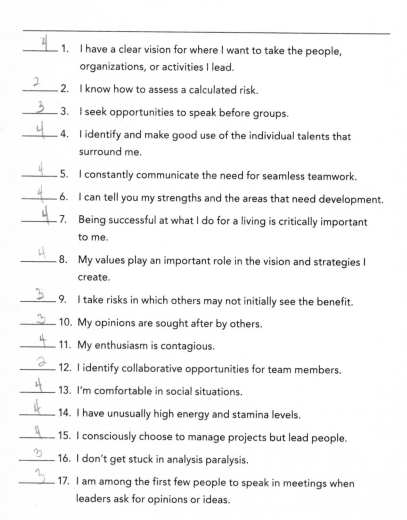

___4___ 1. I have a clear vision for where I want to take the people, organizations, or activities I lead.

___2___ 2. I know how to assess a calculated risk.

___3___ 3. I seek opportunities to speak before groups.

___4___ 4. I identify and make good use of the individual talents that surround me.

___4___ 5. I constantly communicate the need for seamless teamwork.

___4___ 6. I can tell you my strengths and the areas that need development.

___4___ 7. Being successful at what I do for a living is critically important to me.

___4___ 8. My values play an important role in the vision and strategies I create.

___3___ 9. I take risks in which others may not initially see the benefit.

___3___ 10. My opinions are sought after by others.

___4___ 11. My enthusiasm is contagious.

___2___ 12. I identify collaborative opportunities for team members.

___4___ 13. I'm comfortable in social situations.

___4___ 14. I have unusually high energy and stamina levels.

___4___ 15. I consciously choose to manage projects but lead people.

___3___ 16. I don't get stuck in analysis paralysis.

___3___ 17. I am among the first few people to speak in meetings when leaders ask for opinions or ideas.

_3_ 18. I am able to help people see the benefits of doing things they may initially resist.

_4_ 19. I plan team meetings in advance so as to make good use of team members' time.

_4_ 20. I am able to read and respond appropriately to the nonverbal messages of others.

_4_ 21. I exude self-confidence.

_4_ 22. I take abstract ideas and turn them into tangible plans for the future.

_3_ 23. I seek input from others before taking risks but don't over-rely on their opinions.

_2_ 24. My communication style commands the attention of a group.

_2_ 25. I regularly give people both positive and negative feedback.

_2_ 26. I consciously align people behind the team's vision, mission, and goals.

_4_ 27. I exhibit an upbeat and positive attitude even during difficult times.

_4_ 28. I thrive on innovation.

_3_ 29. I analyze data and situations before jumping in to take action.

_1_ 30. I say things others may think but won't risk saying.

_2_ 31. I provide data, facts, and figures to support my suggestions.

_2_ 32. I believe most people strive for excellent performance.

_3_ 33. I ensure that team roles and responsibilities are clear to all team members.

_4_ 34. I monitor my moods and behaviors.

_3_ 35. I am doggedly persistent.

_2_ 36. I question tried-and-true ways of thinking and doing things.

_2_ 37. I would rather err on the side of taking a risk than playing it safe.

_3_ 38. I give my opinion in clear, certain terms.

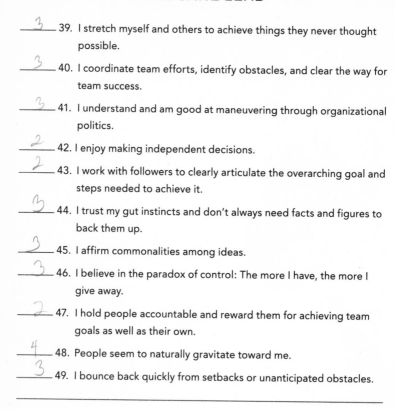

_____3_____ 39. I stretch myself and others to achieve things they never thought possible.

_____3_____ 40. I coordinate team efforts, identify obstacles, and clear the way for team success.

_____3_____ 41. I understand and am good at maneuvering through organizational politics.

_____2_____ 42. I enjoy making independent decisions.

_____2_____ 43. I work with followers to clearly articulate the overarching goal and steps needed to achieve it.

_____3_____ 44. I trust my gut instincts and don't always need facts and figures to back them up.

_____3_____ 45. I affirm commonalities among ideas.

_____3_____ 46. I believe in the paradox of control: The more I have, the more I give away.

_____2_____ 47. I hold people accountable and reward them for achieving team goals as well as their own.

_____4_____ 48. People seem to naturally gravitate toward me.

_____3_____ 49. I bounce back quickly from setbacks or unanticipated obstacles.

Transfer your answers for each question to the corresponding box on the following score sheet. *Add your scores down each column,* then *add each of those scores across for a survey total.* Unlike other surveys, I'm not going to tell you what represents a "good" or "bad" score. A "perfect" score would total 28 in each column, for an overall total of 196. If your score is less than perfect (and believe me, I know *no one* who is perfect), then you've got some areas to work on. Go back and closely examine the category in which you have your lowest score. This is the area that will require your im-

CHAPTER 2 Strategic versus Tactical		CHAPTER 3 Risk Taking		CHAPTER 4 Influence		CHAPTER 5 Coaching		CHAPTER 6 Team Building		CHAPTER 7 Emotional Intelligence and Likability		CHAPTER 8 For the Entrepreneur	
1	4	2	2	3	3	4	4	5	4	6	4	7	4
8	4	9	3	10	3	11	4	12	2	13	4	14	4
15	4	16	3	17	3	18	3	19	4	20	4	21	4
22	4	23	3	24	2	25	2	26	3	27	4	28	4
29	3	30	1	31	2	32	2	33	3	34	4	35	3
36	2	37	2	38	3	39	3	40	3	41	3	42	2
43	2	44	3	45	3	46	3	47	2	48	4	49	3
Total	23	Total	17	Total	19	Total	21	Total	21	Total	27	Total	24

mediate attention. Where is your highest score? This is the area of leadership that represents your greatest strength.

Subsequent chapters correlate with each of the categories on the score sheet. I suggest you first go to the chapter that corresponds with your lowest score and work on the behaviors and coaching suggestions there. Then you can go back and read the other chapters in order of developmental need. Remember, just because you're good at something doesn't mean you can't pick up a few tips from the suggestions provided in *every* chapter.

CHAPTER TWO

If You Can Run a Household, You Can Be Strategic

We still think of a powerful man as a born leader and a powerful woman as an anomaly.

—Margaret Atwood

You've already been strategic if you've:

- Figured out a way to get three kids to three different events on a Saturday and still picked up the laundry, gone grocery shopping, and made dinner for the in-laws.
- Planned a surprise birthday party for your husband or a baby shower for a friend in the midst of traveling on business, meeting tight deadlines at work, and caring for an elderly parent.
- Participated on a nonprofit board charged with the responsibility for turning around an underperforming organization.
- Volunteered to lead a PTA, church, travel club, or some other organization's fund-raiser.
- Mapped out a family vacation, taking into consideration each family member's interests, likes and dislikes, and preferences.

What all these behaviors have in common are a *vision* and a *plan*. Women balance strategy and tactics all the time, but they don't think of themselves as strategic. The first time I was asked to write a strategic plan for my department, I felt my heart begin beating faster as fear coursed through my body. I didn't consider myself strategic, had never taken any classes in strategic planning, and naively prided myself on being a doer, not necessarily a planner. I was at a complete loss for where to start. So I started reading about the subject and learned that I *was* in fact strategic; I'd just never called it that. Strategy is no more complicated than creating a plan for the future and developing a systematic method for achieving it. Women, by virtue of the fact that they have to multitask and manage competing priorities in many aspects of their lives, make superb strategists.

You are strategic. Don't let all the academic articles and big words used by strategists diminish your self-confidence in this arena. This chapter will give you a better understanding of the fundamentals of strategic thinking and planning. But it's not enough to be strategic—you must balance it with tactics or action. Strategy without action is a dream. Action without strategy maintains the status quo. Balancing the strategic and the tactical—something women do quite naturally without even thinking about it—contributes to strong leadership. Simply put, your *strategy* establishes direction. It's a big-picture look at the direction you want to go with a focus on the forest, not just the trees. Your tactics allow you to achieve that direction through specific behaviors, tasks, and milestones.

Dr. Tammy Wong, chief strategy officer for the partner organization of Sun Microsystems, gave me an analogy related to strategic planning that nearly every woman can relate to—losing weight:

> *You simply start with a vision like "I want to be thin" or "I want to be healthy." Then you set your end goal. It might be five pounds or ten pounds. You know you can't do it in a healthy way over*

the course of a week, so you break it down into small steps—what needs to be done to achieve this goal. That usually means reducing your calorie intake and increasing your exercise level. You then develop a plan for doing each of those two things. You might come up with a schedule for walking or working out three times a week or limiting your calories to fifteen hundred per day. These are all elements of a strategic plan—we just don't think of them that way.

GOOD STRATEGIES BEGIN WITH GREAT VISION

When President George Herbert Walker Bush (the first Bush) expressed disdain for the importance of vision with his comment "I don't get this vision thing," he let corporate leaders off the hook. Many interpreted this statement to mean that vision wasn't important. On the contrary, not only is it important—it's *imperative* for good leaders. In fact, the one message expressed by nearly every woman I spoke with about leadership was the need for a clear vision. As former Texas governor Ann Richards told me just before she died, "To be an effective leader, a woman must know what she wants and where she is taking everyone else." Surely that was one of the reasons why Governor Richards was admired by so many people—and not only in Texas.

Many of us will forever remember the late Mary Kay Ash, founder of Mary Kay Cosmetics, as that woman who gave away pink Cadillacs. When she was once chided by a male CEO for this rather unique form of employee recognition (which we'll talk about in a later chapter), she asked in that sugary sweet Southern drawl of hers, "And what color Cadillacs do you give to your employees?" What people don't often think about is the fact that when Mary Kay started her cosmetics business, no one dreamed she would successfully compete with more established companies such as Revlon, Estée Lauder, and Cover Girl. She was a single mom who knew little about cosmetics and even less about running a business. But she had a vision: *to create work for women that would allow them to become financially independent and still allow them to lead lives where God could come first, family could come second, and work could come third.* I wonder how many leaders would want work to come third in the lives of *their* followers?

The vision paid off. She started the company in 1963 with her life savings of five thousand dollars. By 2003, Mary Kay Cosmetics was one of the largest direct sellers of skin care and color cosmetics in the world, employed more than a million Independent Beauty Consultants worldwide, and realized annual revenues of nearly $1.8 billion. You don't have to aspire to such greatness, but you would be foolish not to learn from Mary Kay's story. Strategy and vision go hand in hand. When you want to develop a strategy for increasing the effectiveness of a department, company, nonprofit, school, or household, you've got to make time in your busy schedule for *visioning.*

Author and Harvard professor John Kotter taught me a lot about vision. In his book *A Force for Change,* he describes vision as ". . . not mystical or intangible but simply a description of something (an organization, a corporate culture, a business, a technology, an activity) in the future, often the distant future, in terms of the essence of what it should become. Typically, a vision is specific enough to provide real guidance to people yet vague enough to encourage initiative and to remain relevant under a variety of conditions." Think about that for a moment. *What is your vision for the activity or endeavor you are currently attempting or desiring to lead?* Is it to bring your organization to the next level by developing a new line of products not currently available in the market?

Or perhaps to create systems to strengthen the infrastructure for a nonprofit at which you are a volunteer? Once you have clarity in your vision, you'll be in the business of strategic planning.

Consider the success stories of these leaders who started off with a vision. You may never have considered these women leaders, but they are. They got people to follow them—sometimes to places where people were originally reluctant to go:

- Mother Teresa—to provide care and comfort to the poor.
- Liz Claiborne—to develop a clothing line for the "average" woman.
- Marian Wright Edelman—to establish an organization (Children's Defense Fund) to give voice to the millions of poor children across the United States.
- Gloria Steinem—to get more women involved with politics by founding the National Women's Political Caucus and the Women's Action Alliance.
- Margaret Sanger—to give women more control over their lives by ensuring the availability of safe birth control.
- Rachel Carson—to increase awareness and action related to the irrevocable hazards of pesticides and the connection of all life-forms.

Vision Makes a Difference

Your vision doesn't have to be grand or profound, but without it you can't expect people to follow you. Let me tell you about one woman you've most likely never heard of but who makes a difference in people's lives every day because of her vision for the future. I've had the privilege of knowing and working with Cristina Regalado for more than ten years. I've watched her move from an individual contributor position at the Los Angeles Women's Foundation to her current position as vice president of programs at the California Wellness Association. In this role, she's responsible for managing a team of eight to twelve program directors, overseeing a grant-making budget of $45 million, and maintaining relationships with six hundred grant recipients throughout California.

What I admire most about Cristina is her crystal-clear vision, her ability to communicate it, and her skill in influencing others to achieve it. She came to this country from the Philippines in 1984 and found her way into the field of philanthropy through her own value system and interest in women's rights. Cristina is the perfect example of a woman who has successfully combined her desire to simultaneously "do good" and "do well."

When she assumed her current position, what was in the forefront of her mind was being in a role where she could influence the direction of philanthropic giving at the foundation. She knew she had to be able to articulate a clear and cogent vision if she was to get others to follow her in pursuit of it. Her vision is *to direct money and resources to marginalized and disenfranchised communities so that attention can be brought to the assets they bring to society and the challenges they face.* Cristina works to change the impression many people have that poor people are noncontributors to society—and one way she does this is to give them the tangible resources required to confront poverty. When I asked her the core strength that contributes to her ability to achieve her vision, here's what she told me:

> *My values are what I stand on and harness to create social change. I have a fundamental belief in justice and equality for all. This was probably shaped by my own experience growing up in the Philippines under a dictatorship government. Seeing what*

leads to poverty, how people abuse power, and how people re-sist abused power made me realize change is possible—it's about challenging the status quo.

Being in the world of philanthropy allows me to live my val-ues in a direct, concrete, and strategic way. I have access to power and influence and the ability to use it for good. The way to make change happen is to lead people—to engage them in the process of change. To bring out the talents of the people you lead, you have to start with your values and vision. This is true if you're selling cars or helping to eradicate poverty. Vision is an important directional guide—a compass—that provides a sense of coherence to your daily activities and links what you're doing to something bigger. Leadership is hard, and vision provides me with the inspiration I need. People follow me because they share the vision.

And there we have it again: the kind of values-based vision you need to get people to follow you. Take a moment to think about your own values. They could involve creating new products that benefit humankind, providing high-quality health care to the el-derly, or even developing sound fiscal practices and policies that will ensure your company continues to meet the needs of its em-ployees and the community. In a recent keynote address I gave, I was discussing the importance of vision when someone asked me what my own vision was. Without blinking an eye, I was able to say, "To facilitate significant and enduring change in the lives of the people I am privileged to serve by providing compassion-ate, creative, competent, and courageous coaching." It has been, as Cristina Regalado described, the compass that links what I do every day to my broader belief system.

What are *you* going to say when you're asked the same question? If you haven't already done it, I encourage you to develop your one-line vision statement. It should be a concise reflection of what you do and how you do it. Write it down. Wordsmith it. Practice saying it until it rolls off the tip of your tongue with ease and confidence.

BALANCING THE STRATEGIC AND THE TACTICAL: LEADERSHIP VERSUS MANAGEMENT

To understand the difference between strategy and tactics, you have to understand the difference between leadership and management.

No matter how hard you try, you can't manage people—you *manage* processes and *lead* people. And people will not follow you for long if you don't have a vision and strategy. So what's the difference? John Kotter provides the best description of the difference between leadership and management that I have ever seen. He graciously gave me permission to print the following chart:

THE DIFFERENCE BETWEEN LEADERSHIP AND MANAGEMENT

FUNCTION	MANAGEMENT	LEADERSHIP
Creating an agenda	Planning and budgeting: Establishing detailed steps and timetables for achieving needed results, and then allocating the resources needed to make that happen.	Establishing direction: Developing a vision of the future, often the distant future, and strategies for producing the changes needed to achieve that vision.

FUNCTION	MANAGEMENT	LEADERSHIP
Developing a human network for achieving the agenda	Organizing and staffing: Establishing some structure for accomplishing plan requirements, staffing that structure with individuals, delegating responsibility and authority for carrying out the plan, providing policies and procedures to help guide people, and creating methods or systems to monitor implementation.	Aligning people: Communicating the direction by words and deeds to all those whose cooperation may be needed so as to influence the creation of teams and coalitions that understand the vision and strategies, and accept their validity.
Execution	Controlling and problem solving: Monitoring results vs. plan in some detail, identifying deviations, and then planning and organizing to solve these problems.	Motivating and inspiring: Energizing people to overcome major political, bureaucratic, and resource barriers to change by satisfying very basic, but often unfulfilled, human needs.
Outcomes	Produces a degree of predictability and order, and has the potential of consistently producing key results expected by various stakeholders (e.g., for consumers, always being on time; for stockholders, always being on budget).	Produces change, often to a dramatic degree, and has the potential of producing extremely useful change (e.g., new products that customers want, new approaches to labor relations that help make a firm more competitive).

Once more, your *strategy* establishes direction. It's a big-picture look at the direction you want to go with a focus on the forest, not just the trees. Your *tactics* allow you to achieve that direction through specific behaviors, tasks, and milestones. As I indicated earlier, women are masters at combining the two. Let me give you an example. Let's say your elderly mother, who lives alone in her own home, can no longer care for herself due to the onset of dementia. Your strategy, or the direction you want to go, is to move her into some kind of assisted-living situation where she will be safer. You also know she's not going to go without a fight. So you have to develop a plan (or tactics) that will make the transition less painful for you both. Your tactics might include involving other family members, identifying several facilities and allowing her to choose her favorite, having her identify her most cherished possessions to take with her, and listening to her concerns and providing answers that will make the move more palatable for her. Step by step, you achieve your strategy through clearly identified tactics. You may not have thought that taking such actions are balancing the strategic with the tactical, but they are.

Similarly, let's say you're given responsibility at work to resolve the problem of low employee morale. The first step of your strategy may be to conduct an employee climate survey, then provide recommendations to management. You wouldn't just send out a survey, though; instead, your tactics could include researching various surveys and identifying one that is appropriate for your organization, communicating with employees about the goals of the survey and asking for their cooperation while at the same time managing their expectations, distributing the survey and analyzing the results, then developing a set of recommendations to management based on the findings.

In presenting your findings, you might want to have another strategy, this one for ensuring buy-in at the highest levels by tying the recommendations into the company's vision, mission, and val-

ues. Subsequent tactics would then include categorizing recommendations into each of these three areas, showing a cost-benefit
analysis, providing the report in advance to each person involved
in the decision-making process, calling a meeting to discuss the results, and reaching an agreement on which recommendations will
be pursued. As you can see, whether it's at home or at work, you
first identify the direction, then come up with the steps needed to
move in that direction.

When thinking about women leaders I've personally known who
are both strategic and tactical, one in particular comes to mind: Mary
Ann Chory. She's the director of the multidisciplined engineering
organization at Northrop Grumman Space Technology in Redondo
Beach, California. Mary Ann leads close to a thousand people responsible for designing a variety of cutting-edge products and technolo-
gies such as spacecraft, lasers, rockets, and solar arrays. When I asked
to interview her, she was a bit surprised by the angle I wanted to take.
I didn't want to talk about how she balances strategy and tactics at
work; I wanted to know how she applied the same strategic and tactical skills she used to lead a large group at work to her home life. In
her usual thoughtful and deliberate way, Mary Ann shared her story:

> I always knew I wanted to be both a mom and a professional
> woman—and excel at both. Around the time I had my first child,
> a lot was being written about the "mommy track." It made me
> mad because I thought the term branded me with a scarlet letter.
> Then I realized it didn't have to limit me—it could actually make
> my life less stressful, because it made me think about how steep
> I wanted my professional slope to be. You have to make choices
> about how to create quality in both places. I had to say no to
> certain things. I couldn't travel on business for months on end

when the children were little or take an assignment out of the country. A few months away from the kids when they were less than a year old would cause me to miss a lot of their lives. I was fortunate that I worked for a company that was sensitive to these issues and there really were no long-term negative ramifications, but I still felt as if I was disappointing people at work who were offering me these great opportunities. Picking the right company to work for is important if you want to be able to juggle the kids' needs and your work responsibilities.

Then my husband and I consciously chose a place to live that was close to both of our offices, had good day care, and was a family-friendly neighborhood. The neighborhood was particularly important because I had no family in the area and I wanted to create an extended family and support system.

To stay involved with school and community activities took some planning on my part. I could do it, but I had to be strategic about it. For example, I knew I couldn't volunteer to do things that would require me to be at the school every week at a certain time—but I could chaperone a field trip. These are usually scheduled well enough in advance so I could plan for it. I also volunteered to be on the school sight council—it's a monthly meeting held in the evening where parents and school administrators meet to discuss issues. This gave me the opportunity to learn more about how the system works. It turned out my experience leading large groups of people was really valuable. They looked to me to help facilitate conflicts that arose between the two groups. Just like at work, there were different constituents, and I was good at helping people to see each other's viewpoints. Doing this at the council actually helped me to do it even better at work. I also realized that people who go into education often don't have *the business skills needed to develop strategic plans or benchmark best practices. So I could help in those areas, too.*

My vision was to make a difference and live a multidimensional life. I strategically planned to make it happen. What makes you sane and happy will make your family sane and happy, too.

I hear variations on Mary Ann's story echoed by women leaders around the globe. We live in a society where women bear the burden of ensuring their children are well cared for and nurtured. It's nothing to be apologetic about. You *can* be a leader at home, in your community or schools, and at work, but as Mary Ann found out, it involves knowing what you value most, then combining strategic planning and tactical organization to be able to live (or work) in a way consistent with those values.

VISION, STRATEGY, TACTICS: PUTTING IT ALL TOGETHER

I'd like to end this chapter with a story that beautifully portrays informal but effective leadership that combines everything discussed thus far and in future chapters as well. There's a young woman by the name of Kim Finger who works in my office. If you've ever called and asked to speak with me, or sent an e-mail to me through our Web sites, you were most likely referred to Kim. By title she's the director of client services for Corporate Coaching International and Drloisfrankel.com, but in reality we call her the glue that holds the entire office together. She's worked side by side with me for so long that frankly I don't know what I would do without her. Kim holds a PhD in developmental education from the Claremont School, but that really has nothing to do with how effective she is on so many fronts. Her true passion is unrelated to what she does for a living; it's focused on animal welfare. Her vision is to create local systems and agencies that ensure the humane treatment of animals.

In the aftermath of Hurricane Katrina, we all saw profoundly moving pictures emerging from the devastated areas. I was touched by the human suffering; Kim, however, homed in on the plight of animals, many of whom were dead or dying from neglect, disease, and a host of other factors. She was struggling with what she could do to help when a call came from an animal rescue colleague asking if she would be willing to take in a rescued pet that would be arriving from New Orleans. This was all she needed to put together a strategic plan for rescuing hundreds more animals from the hurricane zone by bringing them to Southern California and finding homes for them—some permanent, some only until their owners could be located. She sent out an e-mail to about fifty people in her network, and within twenty-four hours she'd received five times that many replies. Within forty-eight hours, that had multiplied exponentially. Word was spreading like wildfire through the ether that this animal rescue was under way, and soon she was bombarded with like-minded people wanting to help.

Now came the time for creating tactics to support achievement of the strategic plan. Kim started thinking about how this was going to work *in reality*. A colleague of hers had gotten a wealthy philanthropist to donate an airplane to transport the animals from New Orleans to Los Angeles. What was going to happen when they arrived? Kim made a list of everything that had to be done, including but not limited to feeding the animals, getting the appropriate shots for them, and securing transportation from the airport to the holding facilities. As the list grew, Kim knew that she could not do it all alone. So she clearly told all those in her network through e-mails, blogs, and other electronic forms of communication what she needed and asked for help. People responded to her requests beyond her expectations. Corporate sponsors came forward to donate food and medical supplies, veterinarians donated their time, and animal lovers volunteered their time and homes.

In the face of this overwhelmingly positive response, Kim also knew that she had to maintain volunteer support or it would disappear when she needed it most. So she made certain to provide daily (sometimes more often) updates on what was happening, when it was happening, and where it was happening. She talked to individuals about what *they* wanted to do, not just what *she* needed them to do. Each step of the way, she was conscious of the critical importance of keeping people motivated and making them feel appreciated.

Now, I'd be less than honest if I didn't say there were moments when I was annoyed. Kim tried to do this as much as possible outside the office on her own time, but there were still calls, e-mails, and faxes that interrupted her day job. She would arrive late to the office, surviving on an hour or two of sleep each night—and her work reflected it. Had it continued indefinitely, I would most likely have been left with no alternative but to let her go. But Kim's passion and commitment to animal welfare wouldn't let her give up, and I respect her for risking her own job security to pursue her vision.

And on the fifth day—yes, all this took place over a five-day period—a plane arrived at Los Angeles International Airport with 221 animals, all of which were placed into loving foster care. If you want to know what leadership looks like—it's like this. It's about identifying needs, capitalizing on your passion and the passion of others to address those needs, developing concrete plans for ensuring that those needs are met, and focusing on the human needs of those involved so as to ensure their commitment and cooperation when you need them most. I believe the fact that Kim is a *woman* is what made her so successful at her efforts. She was able to focus simultaneously on the goal, the tactics, and the people to achieve success. It was never about Kim. It was always about the animals and the people. Next time you think you need a title to be a real leader, remember Kim. If you think you have to be rich to lead a major effort, or if you're waiting to be asked before you're willing to step up and lead, remember Kim.

Coaching Tips for Balancing the Strategic with the Tactical

1. **Understand the competitive playing field.** Know what your competitors are doing and be up to date on the best practices in your field. Your vision doesn't have to reinvent the wheel, but it does have to align with your organization's bottom line (in terms of profits, processes, products, or people) for it to be meaningful and add value. Even the most forward-looking vision will be shot down if it's not seen as consistent with the direction your organization is moving. The best way to put this particular coaching tip into practice is to read your company's annual report, talk to executive management about organizational goals, belong to professional associations and read their monthly magazines, and network within your field.

2. **Articulate your vision.** Write down what you want to achieve. Be as specific as possible. Be certain to include what you want to do, how you want to do it, and what people will get out of doing it with you. Here are some examples:
   - To provide internal and external customers with the highest-quality services by eliciting and utilizing the individual and collective talents of our team of highly skilled professionals.

- To protect the company's assets by forging a team of experts who provide timely, accurate, and state-of-the-industry legal advice.
- To create a social service agency devoted to the unique needs of working single mothers and comprising representatives from our constituents who can provide counseling and access to community resources.

3. **Refine and gain support for your vision.** Present your vision to your team and ask for their input. Rewrite it as many times as necessary to ensure that the people who are responsible for making it a reality completely align behind it. Do not become proprietary about your original vision—trust that others will enhance it, not detract from it.

4. **Communicate the vision.** Once you have reached consensus about the vision from your constituents (team, volunteers, colleagues, and so forth), communicate it broadly with posters, on mugs, in performance evaluation forms, and the like. Keep it alive and in the forefront by referring to it in meetings and holding people accountable for achieving it.

5. **Analyze situations before taking action.** Women have the tendency to want to jump in and take action before they completely understand all the facets of a situation. When presented with a challenging situation, use the 5 W's to ask *what, where, why, who, when*:

- What is the deviation from the norm? If things were as they should be, what would the situation look like?
- Where in the organization does the problem lie? Is it an isolated problem or more pervasive?
- Why is it happening? Is there something I'm doing (or management is doing) to contribute to the problem? Is it lack of communication?

- Who is involved with the problem? Whom can I speak with to gain more insight and information?
- When does the problem happen? When does it not happen?

6. ***Develop a clearly articulated strategy.*** Whether it's a problem you're solving or a change in direction you want to undertake, develop your overarching strategy for addressing the challenge. This isn't something you do alone, but rather *with* your followers. It's the best way to ensure their buy-in and commitment to outcomes. Be prepared to discuss your vision or ideas for the general direction, then work with your constituents to come up with the strategy. Examples of strategies include:

- To increase sales by reducing delivery time, developing personal relationships with our customers, and improving inspection systems to identify defective products before they leave the warehouse.
- To decrease attrition of value-added employees by identifying high performers, implementing competitive compensation and pay structures, providing incentive programs, and better understanding and meeting the nonmonetary needs of our staff.
- To be known in the community as the go-to agency for all matters related to nonprofit organization development, consulting, and leadership training.
- To better meet the needs of our patients by empowering the volunteer staff through training, team building, mentoring, and coaching.

7. ***Create a strategic worksheet.*** Once you know *what* you want to do, work with your followers to devise a plan to achieve it. Consider including these key elements:

- What has to be done?
- When is the anticipated date of completion?
- Who will be responsible for overseeing the activity?
- Who else will be involved in achieving the specific goal?
- What are some benchmarks?

On the pages following is an example of what such a worksheet might look like. You can always tailor it to meet your unique needs.

8. ***Identify measures to gauge progress and recognize success.*** When you start your exercise routine or go out to play a sport, you don't just work out until you drop from exhaustion (at least if you're smart, you don't). You have in mind how many repetitions you'll do, how far you're going to run, how long you're going to play tennis, or how many holes you're going to golf. Achieving any goal is much the same. There have to be benchmarks, for you *and* your followers. You can include these on your strategic worksheet or identify with each individual staff member the goals he or she is responsible for achieving. Find the benchmarks by breaking the goal into smaller pieces. If you look at the column "What Must Be Done" on the Strategic Worksheet, you'll notice there are steps involved with each tactic. Each of these is a benchmark that can be measured between the time the task is assigned and the anticipated date of completion. One of the worst things you can do as a leader is to play what author and consultant Ken Blanchard calls "the leave alone/zap," or what Kathleen Booth, director of organizational effectiveness at Warner Bros., calls a "bad game of gotcha!" Both happen when you give people assignments but don't check in with them until the due date. Then, if there's a problem or

STRATEGIC WORKSHEET FOR:
DECREASING ATTRITION OF VALUE-ADDED EMPLOYEES

	WHAT MUST BE DONE	POINT PERSON
TACTIC 1: Identify high performers	Analyze performance reviews; facilitate meetings with senior management; review client feedback forms; form employee steering committee.	Barbara
TACTIC 2: Implement competitive compensation and pay structures	Identify possible external consulting firms; benchmark industry best practices; compare existing structures with industry standards; prepare recommendations to senior management.	Jason
TACTIC 3: Develop on-the-job learning opportunities	Create a leadership university; develop cross-functional teams; partner with external training firms.	Erin

if things are off schedule, you punish them for not meeting your expectations. Not a good way to instill loyalty or confidence in your leadership capabilities.

9. ***Anticipate risks and resistance and plan for them.*** Let me paraphrase one of my favorite quotes from Machiavelli:

WHO ELSE WILL BE INVOLVED	ANTICIPATED DATE OF COMPLETION	OTHER
Joe, Gretchen, Cynthia, Steve	April 22	Inform information systems of data needs (Joe). Communicate goals to senior management (Gretchen).
Anna, Bob, Rick	June 1	Research professional association database (Rick).
Steve	Ongoing	Ask for input from OD department. Research ASTD data base.

There is nothing more difficult than to be a leader who steps up in the face of change. For he will always be met with resistance from those who are better off under the old and only lukewarm acceptance from those who may be better off under the new. Before barging full steam ahead into your strategic plan, talk to people about potential stumbling blocks. Consider whose support you will need in the process, and build alliances with these people. Prepare to overcome objections by learning from the inevitable resistance.

10. **Develop your strategic thinking capabilities by:**
    - Learning to play chess or poker.
    - Consistently asking yourself, *What's the bigger picture here?*
    - Consciously seeking ways to improve existing processes by asking your team to identify ways to do what you already do—*better.*
    - Broadly defining your role. Don't stay in your comfort zone.
    - Holding team brainstorming sessions (preferably with an outside facilitator).

11. **Resist perfectionism.** Thinking that you have to be perfect causes your strategic thinking to be constricted. Strategic thinking involves creativity and harnessing the collective wisdom in the room. Perfectionism also contributes to analysis paralysis and not being able to efficiently implement the tactics you develop. The balancing of strategic thinking and tactical implementation is by nature imperfect.

12. **Be realistic but do take calculated risks.** You don't want to go to the boss and tell her your advertising strategy will cost $3.5 million, take all the time of your staff members for eighteen months, and involve elephants and other circus animals. That would be a bit out of bounds for even the best strategic thinker (even if they may be good ideas). Instead, take into consideration budgets, staffing, and what your corporate cul-

ture can tolerate. Remember, you want to play your game at the edge of the bounds . . . without going too far out.

13. **Look for the relationships between things instead of focusing on one item at a time.** For example, if you're devising a strategic plan for your department, consider the needs of other departments, your constituents, and your followers. Consider how it will create a ripple upstream and downstream. Similarly, when attempting to resolve a problem, don't look at it in isolation. Be sure to delve into potentially related problems and causative factors.

14. **Subscribe to (and read) magazines in your field that address trends and best practices.** Just because strategic thinking isn't your greatest strength doesn't mean you can't find good ideas in books and magazines and incorporate some of these into your own plans.

15. **Dare to be a tall poppy.** This is a phrase I learned from a colleague in New Zealand. It refers to the tendency of people to not want to stand out from their peers. But good leaders *should* stand out. Whether you work for a *Fortune* 500 corporation or a small nonprofit, it's easy to unconsciously fall victim to groupthink. Consider reading *Orbiting the Giant Hairball* by Gordon MacKenzie. This business cult classic is a terrific little book that makes you realize how creativity can be stifled by organizational expectations—and what you can do about it.

CHAPTER THREE

Taking Risks: No More Nice Girl

You gain strength, courage and confidence in every experience in which you really stop to look fear in the face . . . You must do the thing you think you cannot do.

—Eleanor Roosevelt

You've already taken risks if you've:

- Taken the plunge and gotten married.
- Bought a home (extra credit if you're single).
- Changed jobs or career fields.
- Invested in the stock market.
- Taken a high-profile assignment.
- Ever expressed an opinion contrary to the prevailing sentiment in the room.

The theme of the leader as risk taker came up in many of the conversations I had with women leaders. Whether it's taking a job with a larger scope of responsibility or proposing a new way to fund-raise, it's a risk. You lay yourself bare for people to criticize, analyze, and take potshots at. Perhaps no one said it as well as Kim Walsh, vice president for communications with Pacific Gas and Electric Company (PG&E):

To be an effective leader, a woman must move outside her comfort zone. She can't just see herself as a manager or a caretaker—she has to be willing to take risks if she's going to move out of the number two spot. That happened to me when I first came to PG&E as director of media relations. I had been here less than a year, I was pregnant with my third child, and I was given the opportunity to become an officer of the company and head up the entire communications department. My choice was to let them go out and recruit someone else and remain number two or take a risk. I had a vision and I knew where I could take the organization. It was scary, but ultimately I knew I'd rather try and fail than never try at all.

It's not always comfortable to be the one to put a stake in the ground knowing there is a long way to go and the path isn't clear. I do it on a daily basis. You can sit for hours debating the direction, but someone has to say, "We're going." When someone steps up, sets a course, and sets deadlines for achieving it, the team lines up behind it.

Stepping up to the leadership plate is always a risk. A woman's fear, however, is well-founded. Unlike her male counterparts, she knows that she may get only one swing at the ball, her actions will be closely scrutinized, and there are many people (both men and women) who simply do not want to be led by a woman. Why would any woman in her right mind even *consider* it? Because, as Kim Walsh implies, if you don't take the risk, you relegate yourself to being the perpetual bridesmaid and never the bride.

The risks that leadership requires are particularly difficult for women, who so often suffer from the rarely fatal but always limiting "disease to please." They want everyone to like them. They think they need to do everything perfectly. They're inclined to do things by themselves rather than delegate. They don't want to disappoint anyone. Sounds a little like being a new mother, doesn't it? New mothers want to know their babies will one day love them back. They think that if they're not perfect, there will be some catastrophic result. Not wanting to look like they aren't good mothers, they are reluctant to ask for help. And despite all the additional responsibilities that come with motherhood, they try hard to keep up with all their previous activities, too, for fear they will drop a ball and disappoint someone. Again, why would any woman in her right mind even consider motherhood?

Fortunately for all of us, women not only consider it, they take the risk and *do* it. Eventually they learn there is no such thing as the *perfect mother*. Women need to apply this to their roles outside the home and understand there is also no such thing as the *perfect leader*. Leaders are imperfect human beings—and once you realize that, you're on the right path to becoming an even better leader. By definition, taking a risk means not being able to predict the outcome with 100 percent certainty. But not taking a risk means knowing with the same degree of certainty that things won't change.

WOMEN AS RISK TAKERS

In my book *Nice Girls Don't Get Rich: 75 Avoidable Mistakes Women Make with Money,* I talked about the fact that the average woman is less willing than a man to take financial investment risk for financial gain. At the same time, studies show that when women *do* take financial risks, the outcomes exceed those of men. Why? Because when women take financial risks, they do it with more advance planning and stay in their investments longer than men.

Interestingly, another study, conducted by the National Association of Women Business Owners (NAWBO), reveals that women entrepreneurs are *substantially* more likely than men to take risks when it comes to investing in their businesses. Not only do they take risks, but more than 70 percent of those who took a risk to expand their business reported that they were successful in the undertaking.

It's not that women don't take risks, then; clearly, we do. We just do it differently. Consider some of these women in history who took risks to achieve their goals, which in turn benefited the lives of many others:

- **Wilma Mankiller**: Former principal chief of the Cherokee Nation, she was the first woman in history to lead a Native American tribe. Mankiller faced resistance from people who did not want to be led by a woman. Her tires were slashed, and she received death threats, but she prevailed in her vision to bring self-sufficiency to her people. She generated hope in young Native American women that they could one day grow up to be chief.

- **Harriet Tubman**: Known as the "Moses of her people," Tubman risked her own life to help hundreds of slaves to freedom along the Underground Railroad. She later became a leader in the abolitionist movement.

- **Rosa Parks** was instrumental in propelling the civil rights movement forward when she refused to give up her seat to a white rider on the bus.

More recently, three women who took enormous risks by exposing fraud, corruption, and negligence at WorldCom, Enron, and the FBI were named *Time* magazine's Persons of the Year in 2002. Cynthia Cooper, Sherron Watkins, and Coleen Rowley were described as "ordinary people who did not wait for higher authorities to do what needed to be done." That's called *leadership*.

Fortunately for most of us, the risks we take every day are far less than those taken by these admirable women. So what are some of those risks? Consider the following:

- Influencing the boss to go in a direction different from the one he is espousing.
- Supporting raises for your overworked staff when the company has suggested skipping them this year.
- Being the lone voice for a disparate opinion at a meeting of your colleagues.
- Advocating for a direct report who has made mistakes but who you think shouldn't be fired for them.
- Introducing a new policy that you know won't make you popular, but is the right direction for the organization.
- Convincing a client or customer that the service she requested is not the one she really needs.
- Changing jobs rather than comply with something you think is unethical.

Sometimes *not* taking a risk is the biggest risk you take in the workplace. The question is: How do you know which ones you should take and which ones you shouldn't?

FROM GUT INSTINCT TO CALCULATED RISK TAKING

Too often, when a woman *does* take a risk, she doesn't calculate the risk versus profit. Instead, she relies on more subjective factors

such as her gut instinct or what's sometimes called women's intuition. These kinds of feelings can be valid measures of whether a
risk may be worth taking, but you have to *consciously assess* them
and be able to articulate your rationale in objective, business terms.
Not only does this serve to increase the confidence others have in
your decision, but it also bolsters your own confidence that you're
moving in the right direction.

If you have children, you know what I'm talking about. Subjective factors help you protect them from potentially perilous
situations. For example, your sixteen-year-old wants to attend an
all-night party at the home of a friend. Your intuition tells you this
isn't a good idea. At first you may not be able to put into words why
you won't give her permission to attend the party (that's when you
invoke the "because I'm the parent" rationale), but when prompted
you can come up with a list of legitimate reasons. You remember
that this particular friend has lied to you in the past about whether
her parents would be home while your daughter was visiting. You
recall the time a few months ago when you received a call from
another parent expressing concern over the young woman's driving
while under the influence of alcohol. When you asked your daughter how her friend was doing in school, she told you that she'd been
suspended for smoking in the girls' room. The sum total of these
objective factors translates into your apparently subjective decision
not to let your daughter attend the party.

We are observing behaviors, taking in information, and log-
ging the results of our experiences all the time. We may not be
consciously processing that input, but we do store it in our subcon-
scious. It's why gut instinct and intuition can be reliable—but not
in a vacuum. Successful leaders validate seemingly subjective risks
through the use of objective recollections. That's what is known as

taking a *calculated* risk. You can increase your ability to take smarter risks by using the Facts/Feelings Model of Risk Taking developed by Roberta Hill, a principal in Ward-Green & Hill Associates, a management consulting firm located in Ottawa, Canada. You'll notice that it requires you to assess your *comfort level* with the risk along with your *degree of certainty* about the risk's outcomes. It provides a great place to start when considering whether the potential profit outweighs the risk involved with your decisions.

FACTS/FEELINGS MODEL OF RISK TAKING

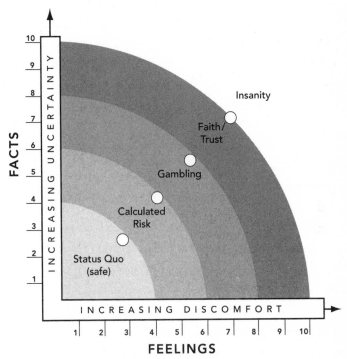

© Copyright 1990, 1997, by Roberta Hill. All rights reserved.

Let me give you an example of how it works. Let's say you're going to buy a used car—a risky undertaking if ever there was one.

Your brother has a car he wants to sell because he was recently provided with a company car. You know that he has owned the car for a little more than a year, he bought it new, it has fourteen thousand miles on it, the warranty is in effect until it reaches fifty thousand miles, and *Consumer Reports* rates this particular model very high when it comes to reliability. On the "Facts" scale, there is little uncertainty. You know what you're getting if you buy the car from your brother. Also, you have a good relationship with your brother and trust that he would not sell you a lemon, you've ridden in the car and liked how it performed, and it's a car you would like to own. So, on the "Feelings" scale, there is little discomfort. Making the decision to actually purchase the car from your brother would then be considered a "safe" risk. Little discomfort + little uncertainty = safe decision.

Now let's change the scenario. Let's say you're considering a job change. You've been with your current company for more than a decade and have topped out in terms of opportunities for upward mobility. It's a small company, and unless your boss leaves (which she doesn't seem to indicate will happen any time soon), there's no place for you to go that would allow you to use your skills and abilities to the degree you would like. You are approached by a competitor who started a similar business across town six months ago. He's familiar with your work and wants to hire you for the same position your boss holds in your current company. He's offered you a 20 percent increase in salary, benefits that are equal to those you have now, and participation in a profit-sharing program, which you don't currently have. In considering whether you should take the career risk and make the move, you are concerned because this is the first business the competitor has started, you do not know how financially stable his company is, and economic indicators suggest that the industry may experience a period of decline over the next eighteen to twenty-four months. On the "Facts" scale, you would rate the uncertainty as a 7.

With regard to your feelings, you are comfortable with not having to make a geographic move or sell your home, you're delighted with the increased pay and benefits, and you genuinely like the man to whom you would be reporting. On the other hand, you're a single mom with total responsibility (financial and otherwise) for three teenage children and like the stability your current company affords you. On the "Feelings" scale, then, you would have to rate the opportunity a 5. Combine this with the relatively high degree of uncertainty about the facts, and you've got a risk level in the "Gambling" category. In the end, you decide you can't afford to gamble at this stage of your life and decide to stay put.

In addition to using the Facts/Feelings model to assess risk, ask these questions to help you make a decision that seems risky:

- What information, data, or experiences do I have that lead me to believe this is a risk worth taking?
- What is the potential profit of taking this risk?
- What is the potential downside of taking this risk?
- What additional information do I need to take a calculated risk?
- Am I willing to accept the consequences if the risk doesn't pan out?
- Whose support do I need to increase the likelihood of a positive outcome?

Is there ever any guarantee that when you take a risk, you'll get the outcome you want? No, but not taking a risk does guarantee you one thing: *Nothing will change.* Risk taking is inherent to every leadership position. Not only do you have the *right* to take risks—it's your *responsibility* to do so. If you simply follow the directives of your management, you're not being a leader. That person is called a functionary—someone who doesn't question the rightness of the direction, but simply complies with orders.

THE COURAGE TO SPEAK THE UNSPOKEN

Risk taking doesn't just involve leadership decisions made about direction, new products, or procedural changes; it also includes the willingness to say difficult things—often things others may be thinking but are afraid to say. Women have far more experience at doing this—and are actually better at it—than they may initially realize. How many times has a girlfriend asked you, "Does this dress make me look fat?" and you had to give her an honest answer? How about when your son comes home with a tattoo and asks you what you think? Or a husband who, in the throes of a midlife crisis, asks for your opinion about taking money out of savings to buy an expensive sports car? Each of these situations calls for the courage to speak the unspoken. In the workplace, at the PTA, or during a family crisis, speaking the unspoken takes the form of giving difficult feedback, disagreeing with proposed directions that will use up time or financial resources better spent otherwise, voicing concern about potentially unethical practices, or proposing new policies that you know will be met with initial resistance.

A woman I consider to be a master at risk taking and speaking the unspoken is Ellen Shedlarz, chief talent officer for Hill & Knowlton, one of the world's largest communications consulting firms. She's held a number of executive positions during her career—and left each organization better for the risks she took while employed there. When I asked her about how and why she takes risks, here's what she told me:

> *The decision to take a risk or not take a risk is about my own personal value system and my ethics. Those are the only two things in life you really own. If something is not fitting within my value system, I feel it's a risk I have to take. An example is when AIDS first came to the forefront and I was working at a company where, like most companies at the time, the philosophy was to ignore it and hope it would go away. I felt we needed to talk about it and teach people about what was becoming an epidemic that clearly wasn't going to go away. I proposed that we train our managers about the issue but did so in a way that showed how it would protect the company—even though my real concern was for the individuals on our staff. As a result, the firm became one of the leaders in managing those diagnosed with AIDS in a respectful and professional way. Being at the forefront of the issue, the firm gained insight into the lives of the people affected.*
>
> *Back then, people with AIDS were trying to sell their insurance policies just to get money to survive, but most companies were paying only pennies on the dollar for them. This was of concern, particularly because we had someone on our staff who was dying of AIDS and needed help. So I looked around the company for people in policy-making positions who I thought would share my values, and together we convinced executive management that we had to do right by the person. As a result of the risk we all took, the company bought his insurance policy dollar for dollar.*
>
> *You've got to figure out the selling point to your audience, find*

people to form alliances with, and anticipate possible reactions. If I think there's going to be a compromise required, I shoot for the moon because that way I have something to give up.

The most important thing with risk taking is to leave emotion out of it and go in with the facts. Facts are friendly. The other thing I do is seek out informal counselors who can help me gain support. That's sometimes even more powerful than just getting the support of your management. Don't wait for an emergency to build your network of informal counselors. As soon as you're in a job, figure out where the informal power is and develop and nurture those relationships, too. It's not just about what they can do for you—you have to figure out what you can do for them.

Not all risks you take will pay off. When they don't, the first thing you have to do is tell your boss. You don't want your boss to find out from someone else. Next, talk to all the players involved and find out what worked and what didn't so you can learn from it. And the last thing is to jump in and do it again.

Values, strategy, and relationships—these are messages you hear again and again from the women leaders with whom I spoke. Whether it's related to developing your vision or taking risks, these are among the factors that make up the fabric of great leaders who take the risk to speak the unspoken.

ELICITING THE INPUT AND SUPPORT OF OTHERS

Another facet of risk taking is making certain you have all the information you need to make a decision—*without* getting bogged down in analysis paralysis. For women, this can take the unique form of something I call polling, or the fear of taking a risk without first finding out what everyone else thinks. At the other extreme is the woman who doesn't ask for input because she's afraid people will accuse her of being gratuitous in her solicitation of their opinions. Here's a real conversation I had with a client who was struggling with gaining input and support without appearing overly dictatorial or solicitous:

Leader: I can't seem to get people on board with this new direction I want to take. Every time I bring it up for discussion at a meeting, there's lots of disagreement about what we should do and the team can't seem to get traction on it.

Coach: Explain to me how you're bringing the topic up.

Leader: Well, I say that I want the team to make decisions about how we should reorganize the department to improve GLP [good laboratory practices]. Then everyone gets into the act advocating for their own position and it becomes a free-for-all where we don't get anywhere.

Coach: Have you thought about making a more affirmative statement about the changes you want to implement, then getting their input on how those can be achieved?

Leader: Then I'll be accused of being too dictatorial. You know how my team is. Everyone wants to have a say about everything.

Coach: Strong teams need strong leadership. At the moment, you're relinquishing your role as team leader to your followers. Advocating for change is never easy, but that's the risk you take as a leader. You can always expect resistance to change and that's not a bad thing. It's the system's way of not throwing the baby out with the bathwater.

Leader: So how do I do that and not get called a dictator?

Coach: By going into the next meeting with a well-planned presentation on the direction you plan to take and asking for the team's input into how to implement the plan efficiently. *You* set the direction, and together you develop the implementation strategies.

Leader: And what do I do when they start shooting holes in my idea?

Coach: Use it to your advantage to fail-safe the new organizational design. Focus the discussion not on *what* we're going to do but *how* we're going to do it. You've got a group of critical thinkers who will find flaws in almost any design. Tell them you *want* them to come up with the potential obstacles to success and suggestions for overcoming those obstacles. Turn it into a problem-solving session, not a critique of your idea.

And guess what? With a healthy degree of skepticism, this leader went to the next meeting prepared to introduce her idea and face the inevitable resistance. She reported back that the meeting went better than she anticipated. People were surprisingly open to the need for change, and she was able to direct their energy into creating a strategic implementation plan. Remember that paraphrase from Machiavelli—*You will always get resistance from those who are better off under the old and only lukewarm acceptance from those who may be better off under the new.* Introducing any kind of change is a risk for the leader. But that's what you get paid for: *to take what's good and make it better; to take what's wrong and fix it.*

CAREER CHANGE: A UNIQUE FORM OF RISK TAKING

One of the best parts of writing this book was the opportunity to interview so many successful and inspiring women. I knew who I wanted to interview, but I didn't always know how they were going to fit into the book when the interviews began. That's why it came as a surprise when I interviewed Alyce Alston, the president of De Beers North America, about risk taking, and she spoke about changing careers as one of the biggest leadership risks she ever took. I realized the same must be true for many women. Whereas a man will assume leadership responsibilities for which he has no specific expertise and assume he will be successful by extrapolating similar experiences, a woman is far less likely to do so. She will turn down opportunities for promotions and assignments that could either develop or contribute to her existing leadership skill set if she thinks she's not 100 percent qualified. I talked about this self-limiting behavior in my book *Nice Girls Don't Get the Corner Office* as one of the impediments to reaching the higher levels of organizations.

The risk Alyce Alston took is one from which many of us can learn. She spent twenty years in publishing in senior leadership positions, including publisher of *W* magazine and *O, The Oprah Magazine*. Although she knew she could remain on her career track in publishing, she also knew she wanted to expand her career portfolio—and she couldn't do that if she didn't take a risk. Here's what she told me:

> *Before moving to De Beers, my husband and I discussed the fact that he just started a new business and with three children one of us had to be the breadwinner, so making a career move would be risky. The older you get, the more risk-averse you become. But financial security never was the real issue for me. The compensation package I was offered wasn't quite what I would have wanted, but the opportunity to learn outweighed the financials. You make compromises for the long run that aren't always*

win-win. *You never really know going in if the risk is going to pay off—that's why it's called a risk. So I said to myself,* What's the worst thing that could happen? *I could always go back to Mississippi if necessary and live quite a good life. I can handle that. It was also possible that I would be able to leverage this move to go on to even bigger things than if I stayed where I was and continued along the same path.*

I love leading companies and businesses and believe that whether it's publishing or retail, much of the process is the same. Coming up with the game plan, hiring the right people, and inspiring and motivating people to achieve it are the same from leadership position to leadership position. But if something is enticing enough and excites you, you should go for it. My feelings come into play now more than in the past. When I didn't trust my gut quite enough and only made my decision intellectually, I wasn't happy.

It's thrilling and exciting and scary all at the same time to make a major shift in industries. It's like starting over. You're really alone in it and have to stay strong. I do that by looking at my past and wondering what I can apply—business isn't about right and wrong but about the process of decision making, and usually the past will help you. Taking the risk to change industries was a humbling experience because I didn't know as much about this business.

Another factor is that you're building new relationships with people who don't know you, so your candor, honesty, and ability to tackle difficult situations is harder. After six weeks in the position I realized I came across too strong and had to shift my style. If I had to do it over again, I would have listened more, observed the culture more, asked more questions, and proceeded differently. It was a real learning experience—but thank goodness for that. It was a valuable lesson I can use forever. When it's hard, I think to myself: This is what makes people good, it's what takes you to the next level—overcoming new challenges and succeeding by building an invigorating and exciting environment. You have to be uncomfortable to grow. *Every day I wish it was easier, but I'm forty-one years old and it's a privilege to go into a new field and learn.*

As you can tell from reading this, Alyce is unique in many ways. Intentionally putting herself in a position and industry where she could possibly fail so that she could grow in the long run is just one way. Her candor is another. There aren't too many executives I know who would be willing to admit they took a lesser compensation package so that they could learn something new. Or that they wish they had listened more, observed more, and asked more questions. I found the discussion of learning from your mistakes particularly interesting: Alyce quickly realized that in a new environment, she couldn't rely on a style that worked when she had strong relationships in place and had already built her reputation.

Shortly after I spoke with Alyce, I had the opportunity to interview another woman I admire, Debra Langford, executive director for strategic sourcing and talent management with Time Warner. How these two women have approached career change is strikingly similar. If you've never considered yourself a risk taker, then you're going to love Debra's story. I met her when *Black Enterprise* magazine was doing a story about my book *Nice Girls Don't Get the Corner Office.* She was one of four women the editors selected to ask whether she'd made any of the mistakes I'd written about. By sheer coincidence, I was giving a presentation at Warner Bros. the same week the article came out, and Debra made a point of introducing herself. I loved her energy, enthusiasm, and unique perspective on most issues—which is why I wanted to speak with her for this book.

Although she was willing to have me interview her, she was a little surprised that I wanted to include her in the chapter on risk taking. As she said at the beginning of our conversation, "I *have* taken risks, but I'm risk-averse." The more we talked, the more abundantly clear it became that her unique brand of risk taking is made more comfortable by the relationships she has built throughout her career. Her story teaches us that you can have all the information you need and feel good about your direction—but if you don't have the people around you to support those decisions, the best-laid plans can quickly turn on you.

> *Women of color take risks all the time, because we are often the first one in our families or circles to have careers within specific companies or industry. We go in without the benefit of a network or preexisting relationships to help us navigate the politics and land mines, or—sadly—even a group to celebrate our wins when we join a company.*
>
> *With that said, the biggest risks I've taken have to do with going out and meeting people, not knowing how I would be received. It's a risk to think that in formal situations, just because I have the right title or work for the right company, the playing field is level, because it's not.*
>
> *A turning point for me was when I went to an entertainment industry NAACP luncheon only to find the table I was to be seated at had a group of African American executives who were huddled together and not interested in having me join their discussion. The safe choice would have been to move to another*

table of people who looked like me, but I didn't. I turned to my left and had a delightful conversation with two gentlemen who, I found out at the end of the lunch, were entertainment industry legends William Hanna and Joseph Barbera. That was a risk that paid off with a job offer at the conclusion of the luncheon, and the beginning of my taking even more risks in terms of career interests in areas where I had no background—only faith that I could succeed if given the chance.

The position I'm in now, identifying women and executives of color for the largest media company in the world, required a huge risk. I had been on the creative side of the entertainment business for seventeen years, overseeing the creative elements for television shows such as The Fresh Prince of Bel Air, Growing Pains, Night Court, China Beach, and MadTV. When I learned about this position, I knew I'd be going into a corporate role with no experience in executive search or recruiting and, to be honest, in an industry where diversity had been an item of interest but not particularly well known for taking action on it. After I interviewed for the job, I was told by the hiring executive that instead of a full-time position, she wanted to make this a one-month consulting opportunity. I negotiated for a three-month term and left a senior vice president job to take the position.

On one hand, it was the biggest risk I ever took. I considered the senior vice president of human resources for Warner Bros. a mentor and true supporter of mine. He told me to trust him— and I did. I knew he believed I could do this job. So in honesty, it was more of a calculated risk. As much as I had his support and the support of many others, I still had to make good.

It was the smartest move I've made. I didn't have what the job description wanted. I'm not a human resources, executive search,

*or OD professional, but I had a reputation for connecting people
and knowing who they are, not just their titles. For the company,
I think it could have been seen as a risk to put me in a new and
ambitious role. The good news is, with my network of supporters,
along with my internal and external relationships, I've been able
to make key introductions of top diverse and female executives,
resulting in more than seventy hires for the company.*

Time and again you'll hear me talking about the importance of
relationships. Alyce learned the hard way that if you start out lack-
ing industry relationships, it's critical to build them before assuming that what worked in the past will work in the future. Debra, on
the other hand, used her existing relationships to ensure success.
Women are often hesitant to capitalize on relationships—they
feel it's somehow taking advantage of people. Remember, there's a
quid pro quo (something in exchange for something else) inherent
in every relationship. If you're keeping up your end of the deal by
providing good service, information, or even friendship, you can
call on the people in your network to help you out when you most
need it.

AND WHEN YOU FAIL . . .

As Ellen Shedlarz points out, failure is inevitable for risk tak-
ers. Why do you think so many successful people are quoted about
failure?

- "Flops are a part of life's menu and I'm not a girl to miss out
  on any of the courses." —Rosalind Russell
- "Failure is the opportunity to begin again—more intelligently." —Henry Ford

- "I've not failed. I've just found 10,000 ways that won't work."
  —Thomas Edison

Not every risk you take is going to pay off the way you wanted it to. But one thing I know about human beings is that they have a deep capacity for forgiveness—with certain caveats. Look at Carly Fiorina, the ousted CEO of Hewlett-Packard. She landed on her feet. Then there's Martha Stewart. Literally and figuratively, her stock is on the rise. Even Bill Clinton's impeachment didn't stop Americans from keeping him in office.

As I said, there are some caveats. When the risk you took outweighed the profit, here are the things you must do to recover:

- **Acknowledge the failure:** The ability to step forward and say "It didn't work but it was worth the try" goes a long way toward redemption. The greater the confidence you have in this acknowledgment, the less likely people are to see you as a failure.

- **Critique it, learn from it, and stay out of the blame game:** Studies show that when a woman fails, she's likely to blame herself. When a man fails, he's likely to blame others. Neither is the best route toward reestablishing your credibility. Others are more likely to be forgiving when they know you were able to look at the mistake without pointing fingers and analyze what went right, what went wrong, and what you will handle differently in the future. Be prepared to do just such an analysis immediately following your failure and communicate the lessons learned to all those whose confidence you want to rebuild.

- **Separate the act from the actor:** Failure is an act, not a person. *You* are not a failure; a risk you were bold enough to take didn't work out. If you internalize messages about being a failure long enough, you will eventually become those messages.

- **Use a success continuum:** We often tend to think in black-and-white terms about our successes and failures. In fact they fall along a continuum of success, from wildly successful to not successful. Measure outcomes as the degree of success rather than the degree of failure.

- **Develop resilience:** Your leadership capability is judged in part by how you respond to failure. If people see you bounce back confidently, they will ascribe to you a critical leadership trait: *resilience*. But don't confuse denial of your feelings or keeping a stiff upper lip with resilience. An emotional reaction that matches the severity of the failure is human. To dwell on those emotions or use them as an excuse for not moving forward is another story.

- **Keep taking calculated risks:** If you stop taking risks because one didn't work out, then you will be allowing that mistake to define you. We all know Thomas Edison was a prolific inventor—but he was also a failure at many things he tried. This didn't stop him from continuing to take the risks needed to go on to other successes.

- **Maintain perspective:** Most of us tend to remember our flops more than our successes. That's one reason why I have an "atta gal" file. It's where I keep notes and other forms of acknowledgment from readers, clients, and colleagues praising me for doing something particularly well. When my risks turn into failures, I pull out this file to remind myself that one failure does not a loser make.

I'd like to end this chapter with a story about resilience. Early in my career as an entrepreneur, I lost a fairly large contract and had no idea why. I asked the client if there was a problem, and she told me they'd simply decided to go in another direction. Try as I might, I could not figure out what I had done wrong. I began to question if I was in the right field and if I was really having the kind of impact I wanted to with my clients. I pulled out my "atta gal" file and it helped somewhat, but the issue was still weighing on my mind when I had lunch with a colleague. As I described the situation to her, she could sense I was feeling pretty down about it. So she shared with me a story that I've never forgotten—and that I pass along to others when they need to hear it most:

> There was once a barnyard filled with lively animals. They were all quite competitive, and it wasn't unusual for them to have contests. One day the resident crow challenged a bluebird to a singing contest. I know I can win this, thought the bluebird. I've worked hard at perfecting a beautiful voice. Together the bluebird and the crow chose the barnyard pig to be the judge of the contest. The bluebird went first, singing her little heart out in a lovely, lilting tune. All the other animals applauded and nodded. Then the crow sang—in the way that crows usually do. Polite applause followed. After thinking about it for a few moments, the pig announced, "And the winner of the contest is ... the crow!" With this, there was an audible gasp in the crowd and the bluebird broke into tears. As the other barnyard animals began leaving the contest area, a sparrow came up and put his arm

around the bluebird. "Don't cry," he said. "We all thought you should have been the winner of the contest." To which the bluebird replied, "I'm not crying because I lost the contest. I'm crying because I let myself be judged by a pig."

Coaching Tips for Taking Risks

16. **Assess your risk orientation.** People have different levels of comfort with risk taking. If your level is too low, you won't take the risks needed to add value to your company. If it's too high, you may be taking foolish risks, gambling with the organization's resources, or causing yourself to be viewed as a loose cannon. When using the Facts/Feelings Model of Risk Taking, if you tend to make decisions that keep you in the "Status Quo" area, you're probably not taking enough risk. On the other hand, if your decisions are often at the "Gambling" level or above, you may be impetuous and not taking enough time to gather the data needed to determine the viability of your decision.

17. **Get in the risk game.** If you're one of those people who always play it safe, you've got to exercise your risk muscle. You can do this by taking small personal risks and learning that the results are rarely catastrophic. The next time someone asks for your opinion, and you know it's contrary to that person's viewpoint, risk putting your perspective on the table rather than taking the path of least resistance by agreeing or saying you have no opinion. When you're in a meeting with people who tend to be more verbal than you are, risk jumping into the debate rather than waiting for just the right moment. There are plenty of ways in which you can gradually move beyond your self-imposed comfort zone.

18. **Qualify and quantify your gut instincts.** You'll approach risk more confidently if you can articulate legitimate business reasons why you think the risk is necessary and will work. Draw on your observations, data, and experiences to develop a rationale for taking risks. The old-fashioned technique of making two lists—one with the potential profits from a decision, the other with its potential downside—works just fine.

19. **Align risks with organizational mission, goals, and values.** Taking risks that don't support the direction the organization wants to go is a setup for failure. No matter how good your idea may be, it will be harder to gain the support you need to ensure success (and you may even find your efforts being sabotaged) if others view it as too closely aligned with your personal needs, not the organization's.

20. **Take calculated risks.** Not all risks are created equal. Calculating the level of risk involves a thorough examination of your comfort level with the risk and with the predictability of outcomes. You should also ask yourself the simple questions included in this chapter to help you delve deeply into the risk-versus-profit equation.

21. **Build in wiggle room.** Most decisions that involve risk don't have to be *either-or.* Men tend to understand this better than women and cut themselves a wider berth to ensure that outcomes will be viewed in the most positive light. We, on the other hand, narrowly define successful outcomes; when we fall short, we feel we have failed. When identifying desired outcomes resultant from a risk, learn instead to create a range of acceptability. For example, if you're about to implement a new payroll system that you influenced your company to buy, it would be unrealistic to expect that it would roll out without

problems. So rather than say, "Implementing this new system will reduce processing time by 20 percent and errors by 40 percent," cut yourself some slack and change that to "Within the first nine months of operation, we will see a decline in processing time of 20 percent, and a 40 percent decline in errors." This way, when the bugs are revealed during the first few payroll cycles, you can legitimately say, "We built in a nine-month window to make this fully operational," rather than feel as if your risk isn't paying off.

22. ***View taking no risks as a potential risk.*** Remaining in your comfort zone or below the radar screen isn't necessarily the best career strategy for leaders. By definition, leaders create change—and that's *always* risky. Increase your risk tolerance by taking small risks where the likelihood of success is good. This adds currency to your credibility account so that when you take bolder risks that don't pan out, you still have the respect and confidence of your management.

23. ***Choose the hill you're willing to die on.*** If you tend to take more risks than your colleagues or are seen as the "conscience" of your organization for continually voicing what others are thinking but aren't willing to say, it could be that you're making mountains out of molehills. Eventually this will label you as a loose cannon—or leave you unable to distinguish important issues from smaller ones. When faced with a host of concerns you'd like to express or changes you want to make, choose the two or three that will make the greatest difference in your ability—and that of your followers—to add value.

24. ***Elicit input and support before taking risks, but don't over-rely on polling or get stuck in analysis paralysis.*** Ultimately you are responsible for the risks you take—no one

else. Input and support can increase the likelihood of success, but they don't take the place of decisive leadership. Similarly, waiting too long to make a decision for fear of making the wrong one will be interpreted as the inability to make any decision. Gauge your sense of urgency on the situation and the urgency level of your management.

25. ***Distinguish between reversible and irreversible risk.*** There are no guarantees of outcomes when you take a risk. That's why you need to know on the front end what will be acceptable to you and what won't. An example of an acceptable reversible risk might be deciding to transfer your investment portfolio to a new financial adviser based on recommendations and research that you've conducted into the manager's track record. You're comfortable with knowing that the new adviser may do worse than your current one, but she may also do better—hence the willingness to take the risk. You plan to stay closely involved with the adviser's decisions and to carefully review all reports and trade activity so that if there is a downward change in the portfolio, you can quickly take action. On the other hand, an unacceptable irreversible risk is one that takes control out of your hands. Let's say you're looking for a new job, and there's a company you've been wanting to work for. A recruiter calls you indicating that the company has an interest in you. If you're offered the position, though, it would require moving to a city where you have no network or support system. The timing is perfect, and it seems like a potentially good move. Then you begin reading about financial problems the company has recently encountered. Their CFO has been fired for fraudulent accounting practices, and the stock has begun to drop. If you leave your current job,

you know there's no going back. You are a single mom of two young children living in a town with a large extended family. Should you take the job, you have no control over whether the company fails or downsizes; you could be left with no job or support system in a new town. You might deem this an unacceptable irreversible risk.

26. **_Plan to fail._** Sooner or later, we all take risks that fail. Being psychologically prepared to cope with this will form the foundation of your resilience—an important leadership trait. When a risk doesn't pay off, the three most important things to do are to accept responsibility without assigning blame, identify what you've learned from the mistake, and articulate those lessons to a management that will be anxious to know you can extrapolate from them to the future.

CHAPTER FOUR

Influencing With (and Without) Authority

The best impromptu speeches are the ones written well in advance.

—Ruth Gordon

You've already been influential if you've:

- Convinced an elderly parent to move to a nursing home.
- Introduced and implemented a new company policy or procedure.
- Raised children who are drug-free.
- Gotten a resistant husband or partner to attend a concert, ballet, or play.
- Negotiated for a lower price on a new car.
- Asked for and received a raise, promotion, or new assignment.
- Written an article or position paper.

For centuries, women have influenced the course of history—not always as the people with formal power, but as the ones who effected change through their words and deeds. Condoleezza Rice, Dr. Elizabeth Blackwell, Margaret Sanger, Eleanor Roosevelt, Coretta

Scott King, and Madeleine Albright are but a few women who never held elected office or the position of corporate CEO, but who nonetheless made significant contributions to society using their influence skills. Women are much more influential than they give themselves credit for. From influencing a child to do the right thing to influencing a colleague to try out a new vendor or procedure, women are quite naturally master influencers—they just don't see themselves as such. One of the things that makes us so good at it is that we frequently remove ego (ours, that is) from the equation. We don't try to *push* others in a particular direction; we try to *pull* them toward our ideas. Push takes muscle. Pull takes influence.

With this said, I also believe that most women could do a much better job of employing influence strategies in their daily communications. Precisely because we do tend to have a better grasp of language than men, we tend to rely on our ability to communicate fluently as opposed to holding our tongues until we can convey our messages in a manner that best suits the situation or the person or group we're attempting to influence. The models provided in this chapter are designed to give you frameworks into which you can put messages that will increase the likelihood of walking away with what you want—whether that's a raise, more resources, or acceptance of an idea or suggestion.

Perhaps the most influential message I've ever read came from an illiterate but articulate slave named Sojourner Truth. The year was 1851, and the place was the Women's Rights Convention in Akron, Ohio. After several men in attendance tried to claim the superior intellect of men, Truth rose to speak. There were women in the audience who tried to stop her, fearing that the women's movement would be tainted by the abolitionist movement. Little did they know that these two movements would be inextricably entwined over the course of history—and that one would actually help the other. Truth couldn't be stopped, and gave what has become known as the "Ain't I a Woman" speech:

> Well, children, where there is so much racket there must be something out of kilter. I think that 'twixt the negroes of the South and the women at the North, all talking about rights, the white men will be in a fix pretty soon. But what's all this here talking about? That man over there says that women need to be helped into carriages, and lifted over ditches, and to have the best place everywhere. Nobody ever helps me into carriages, or over mud-puddles, or gives me any best place! And ain't I a woman? Look at me! Look at my arm! I have ploughed and planted, and gathered into barns, and no man could head me! And ain't I a woman? I could work as much and eat as much as a man— when I could get it—and bear the lash as well! And ain't I a woman? I have borne thirteen children, and seen most all sold off to slavery, and when I cried out with a mother's grief, none but Jesus heard me! And ain't I a woman? Then they talk about this thing in the head; what's this they call it? [A member of the audience whispers, "Intellect."] That's it, honey. What's that got to do with women's rights or negroes' rights? If my cup won't hold but a pint, and yours holds a quart, wouldn't you be mean not to let me have my little half measure full? Then that little man in black there, he says women can't have as much rights as men, 'cause Christ wasn't a woman! Where did your Christ come from? Where did your Christ come from? From God and a woman! Man had nothing to do with Him. If the first woman God ever made was strong enough to turn the world upside down all alone, these women together ought to be able to turn it back,

and get it right side up again! And now that they is asking to do it, the men better let them. Obliged to you for hearing me, and now old Sojourner ain't got nothing more to say.

How I wish I could have been there in person to hear Sojourner Truth deliver her message. I've read it dozens of times, and it never fails to inspire me. But why? What did this woman intuitively know about influence that we can all learn from? Aside from the actual content of her speech (the verbal message), it contains certain elements that are common to all influential leaders—with and without formal authority:

- It reflects her values.
- She expresses herself in straightforward terms using simple words.
- The key message is restated several times using one memorable phrase.
- It contains examples to which everyone can relate to or at least comprehend.
- She knew when to stop, and she let her audience know when she was finished.

I also asked my dear friend and colleague Tom Henschel, president of Essential Communications in Sherman Oaks, California, to read it and tell me, from his perspective as a communications coach, what he thought makes this communication so powerful. This was Tom's response to me:

There are six elements I would point out. Two of them feel specific to the times. But I think that being specific to the times is actually one of its own elements—she knew her audience and used elements that she knew would be effective with them. This is an important aspect of influence—building a relationship with your audience and appearing to be like them or at least understand them. That relationship is no small thing. In addition, here are the five other things I noted.

1. **She begins with a down-home style.** *("Where there is so much racket there must be something out of kilter.") She doesn't speak that colloquially anywhere else in this communication. I believe that was intentional—even if it wasn't on a conscious level. It was tone setting.*

2. **She moves very quickly to the personal.** *She briefly talks about general groups (Negroes of the South, women of the North, and men), but it is very brief. Almost immediately she makes it about herself. It is full of I statements. It's personal. She owns this speech!*

3. **She is passionate.** *No question about that!*

4. **She builds.** *Her first examples are about societal niceties: lifting over ditches, et cetera. Then she elevates to work, then elevates to the lash, then elevates to child loss, then elevates to religion—which, in the mode of the day, was as high as you could go. No earthly thing could trump the holiness of God.*

5. **She sets up a repetitive refrain.** *("Ain't I a woman?") This is like a drumbeat. It is an ancient rhetorical device. It is in Greek literature and Shakespeare and even in Lincoln ("of the people, by the people, for the people"). And Martin Luther King used it so effectively in his "I Have a Dream" speech.*

What we will never know is how long Sojourner Truth sat in her seat and mentally prepared that message. Perhaps she had been mentally preparing it her entire life. We know she didn't write it down, because she was illiterate. But I do know that influential people prepare for every presentation they make—and *every time you open your mouth, it's a presentation.* Why do you think "When E. F. Hutton talks, people listen"? Because he doesn't open his mouth until he's certain of what he wants to say. And people will listen to you, too—if you simply think about what you want to say and the best way to say it before conveying your message.

GETTING TO THE POINT

I was once coaching a woman who tended to think out loud a lot—I mean *a lot.* She's a brilliant woman, but it was difficult to follow her train of thought and glean the most important things she wanted me to know. When I commented on it, she laughed, stood up from the table where we were sitting, and went to her desk to pull something out. She showed me a little booklet that was clearly made by a child in first or second grade. Each page had a statement related to some aspect of his life that the child was to complete. There were statements like "I know my mommy loves me because _____" and "On Saturday my daddy and I _____." She turned to one page, and when I read what her son had filled in I just roared with laughter. It said, "My mommy can't *stop talking*." Out of the mouths of babes comes some of the most meaningful feedback you'll ever receive.

So many women face this exact dilemma. Women tend to give a lot of information in advance of getting to the point. Some do it because they're unsure of themselves; others because they feel compelled, for the sake of fairness, to tell everything they know about a subject before expressing an opinion. *No one wants or needs to know everything that's in your head.* You may feel a need to say it, but it will inevitably diminish your ability to influence effectively.

Tom Henschel uses a model he calls Headline Communication. Not only do I use it myself, but I think it's so valuable that I regularly include it in my coaching with clients. The premise is simple: *The first thing that comes out of your mouth has to be the key message you want people to take away.* The following diagram shows you how to mentally "script" your message in advance.

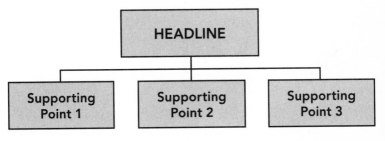

Whether it's a question you're asked or an opinion you want to offer, you'll be considered more credible if you format your communication using this model. Here's how it works. Let's say you're in a meeting where the question is posed: "What's the most important thing we need to do in the next sixty days to overcome the obstacles we're currently facing in the area of product delivery?" This may be the opening you were looking for to get some of your ideas on the table, so the answer could be on the tip of your tongue. Nonetheless, before you open your mouth, think about the headline you want others to hear, and then two or three reasons why you believe this. Once you get used to using the model, it will take you only seconds to formulate your thoughts. Then you can respond with something like this:

HEADLINE
The most important thing we can do is decrease delivery time while increasing productivity quality. There are three ways to do this:

Supporting Point 1	Supporting Point 2	Supporting Point 3
First, we're spending a lot of time processing returns due to problems with quality. That drains our delivery resources. My recommendation is to do a study of why people are returning merchandise and focus on improving in those areas.	Next, we need to consider outsourcing deliveries to locations more than a hundred miles from our manufacturing plant. Given our current staff, we can't guarantee timely delivery.	Finally, we should consider an incentive program that rewards employees for simultaneously reducing errors and delivery time.

Putting your thoughts into this format does something else—it lets *you* know when you've completed your message and gives you the cue to stop talking. If you're not sure you've gotten your point across, don't continue to talk. Instead, ask something like, "Have I answered your question?" This allows others to ask you for further explanation if needed. If so, go back to the model to answer any resulting questions.

Headline Communication isn't appropriate only for the workplace—it's appropriate *everywhere* you want to make a point that gets heard:

- **At home:** I suggest we start planning now for our vacation next summer. It will allow us to get the best airfares, secure a good hotel using our frequent-flier miles, and research the cities we'll be visiting.

- **With friends:** I'd like to see if we could develop a ride-share program for taking the kids to school. This would give each of us at least one day per week we don't have to drive, make certain the kids get to school safely, and get to know a little more about the friends they're spending time with.

- **As a volunteer:** I propose we identify the skills we need to complement our existing knowledge base before we kick off our volunteer drive. This will ensure we have all the skills we need to meet the challenges of running our organization, increase the likelihood of having more diversity on our board, and make people feel as if their unique capabilities will be used if they join us.

Communicating in headlines isn't as difficult as it might initially seem, but it does require forethought. To be influential, regardless of the arena, be certain *before* you begin speaking that you've identified the most important thing you want people to take away from your message.

ASSERTIVE INFLUENCE

When it comes to influence, many women are reluctant to be as straightforward as the examples above for fear of being called the dreaded B-word by their friends and colleagues. It's one reason why we tend to use more words when fewer would do. Using more words always softens your message—and that's *exactly* what women often unconsciously try to do. The obvious problem is that you can't be influential by unnecessarily softening your message. If you've heard me speak or read any of my other books, you know that I view this name-calling as simply a function of the white male system attempting to maintain status quo. Even when you're not expressing yourself inappropriately, you get called names because you're a threat to the direction *they* want to take.

So just how *do* you offer a strong opinion and reduce the likelihood of being called names? It's actually not that hard, but first you have to understand that there are different rules for men and women when it comes to speaking the unspoken. We expect women to exhibit *inclusive behavior*—showing concern for and eliciting the opinions of others rather than simply making declarative statements. Let me give you an example of the difference:

- **Declarative statement:** *I strongly recommend that we change our marketing strategy by the end of second quarter or risk losing a significant portion of our market share.*

- **Declarative + inclusive statement:** *I strongly recommend that we change our marketing strategy by the end of second quarter or risk losing a significant portion of our market share. Now, you can hear that I have strong feelings about this, but I would like to be sure we have everyone else's opinion on the table as well before making a final decision.*

Whereas the first statement leaves no room for discussion, the second openly invites it. It's one of the techniques you can use to disagree without being thought of as disagreeable. The idea here is not to lose your voice or presence in meetings, but rather to add a tagline that increases inclusivity—something expected of women in most cultures. Interestingly, this technique is at the heart of assertive communications, yet when women do it they often feel as if they're being too aggressive.

The following model clearly illuminates how assertiveness is characterized by a combination of high self-expression and high concern for the needs and opinions of others. Based on this model, women are far more likely to act assertively than men—yet when they do, they get called aggressive! Assertiveness is a stereotypically feminine behavior, whereas aggressiveness is a stereotypically masculine one. That's why when you're at your assertive best and are still accused of being too opinionated, you've got to hold your ground, knowing that you've done nothing wrong—and more likely you've done everything right, or you wouldn't pose such a threat.

THE ASSERTIVE LEADER

High Self-Expression + Low Concern for Others = Aggressive Appropriate in emergency situations	**High Self-Expression + High Concern for Others = Assertive** Appropriate in most situations
Low Self-Expression + Low Concern for Others = Passive-Aggressive Never appropriate	**Low Self-Expression + High Concern for Others = Passive** Appropriate in high-risk situations

SELF-EXPRESSION

CONCERN FOR OTHERS

Let me give you a scenario that will illuminate how the different behaviors play out in a situation many of us have experienced. You're in an expensive restaurant and order a steak medium rare. When it arrives and you cut into it, you see it's been cooked so well that it's difficult even to get your knife through it. You have several choices for what to do. If you're:

- **Passive:** You eat the steak, and when the waiter comes over to ask how your meal is, you say, "Just great."

- **Passive-aggressive:** You move the food around on your plate and grumble to your dinner companions about how awful it is. When the waiter comes over to ask how your meal is, you smile and say it's fine. But when the time comes to figure out the tip, you stiff the waiter for not bringing your steak as you requested. As you're leaving, you may even mention to a couple on their way in that they should rethink their choice of restaurant.

- **Aggressive:** You loudly shout for the waiter and in a voice everyone in the restaurant can hear, say, "Does this steak look medium rare to you? Just take it away. I don't know how you people get away with charging this much for a meal."

- **Assertive:** You realize a mistake has been made and quietly signal for the waiter, point out that the steak is not as you had requested, and ask him to bring you another one prepared medium rare. Provided the mistake is correctly promptly and without attitude, you tip him appropriately.

As you can see, each example reflects a greater or lesser degree of self-expression and concern for the other person. Now let's say you have an employee who comes to you and asks for feedback about her performance. She's genuinely concerned about meeting your expectations and is looking for coaching from you. Here's how each type of behavior would sound:

- **The passive leader:** "You're doing just fine. Nothing to worry about. Keep up the good work." The employee is given a good performance review but is missing out on the opportunity to develop new skills that will add to her career mobility. This boss avoids giving honest feedback but doesn't penalize the employee for it.

- **The passive-aggressive leader:** "You're doing just fine. Nothing to worry about. Keep up the good work." Then, when the employee is given her performance review, there are negative remarks and a low rating that cause her to receive a smaller raise than she'd anticipated, given that she was told she was doing a good job. This boss definitely did not have the courage to speak the unspoken. Passive-aggressive leaders often say one thing to the employee's face but another behind his or her back. It makes them difficult to trust.

- **The aggressive leader:** "Are you thick? How many times have I told you that you're going to have to flesh out—obesely flesh out—the details on your write-ups if you ever expect to get ahead around this place? What do I have to do, write it on an engraved invitation?" This boss is certainly high on the self-expression scale but low on concern for others. The employee knows where she stands, but the boss's comments aren't really helpful to her development, and are damaging to her self-confidence.

- **The assertive leader:** "I'm glad you asked. I do have some feedback that might be helpful to you and with a little effort I think you can move your performance rating up from good where you were last year to above average this year. There's one area in particular that I'd like to help you with. First, I noticed your write-ups often contain typos and numerical errors. Reviewing these more thoroughly before submitting them would take care of that problem. You might also consider having one of your colleagues give them a quick review—sometimes a second set of eyes is helpful." This boss gives honest and direct feedback without demolishing the ego of the employee. In other words, she shows high self-expression combined with high concern for others.

With a little practice and mentally preparing your communications in advance, you can develop an influence style that will allow you to express yourself clearly and reduce the likelihood of name-calling.

INFLUENCE WITHOUT AUTHORITY

It's one thing to influence when your position supports it—that is, when you're in charge of a project or department. It's another thing to influence when you have no direct authority to do so. My experience working with people (primarily women) in support positions at professional service firms has taught me a lot about how to influence without authority. That's why I asked Terry Monahan, someone I think has had some of the toughest leadership challenges in business, to share her story with you. For the past twenty years, Terry has led the administrative staff for various offices of McKinsey & Company—considered by many the premier international consulting firm. What makes her job so tough is that although she supervises teams of highly skilled and educated administrative professionals, these people actually take much of their day-to-day instruction from the firm's consultants. In other words, she's the middle person. If a consultant is unhappy with the work of a particular administrative assistant, he or she is likely to go to Terry to resolve the problem. Similarly, if the administrative assistant has a concern about a consultant, Terry is the point person. She constantly finds herself in the position of having to influence people over whom she has no authority. She conducts performance reviews (with input from consultants), provides day-to-day feedback and coaching, and is responsible for motivating a diverse team of men and women. Simultaneously, she must ensure the work performed is up to McKinsey's high standards and meets the expectations of the consultants. Believe me, it's no easy task.

Many women find themselves in similar roles. Perhaps you lead a group of volunteers who are only there out of the goodness of their hearts and over whom you feel you have no real leverage. Or you might even be in a marriage where the kids play you and Dad against each other, and they know Dad will have the final say, causing you to struggle to maintain your credibility. If you're in a position that feels like you're between a rock and a hard place, take a lesson from Terry Monahan. I've observed Terry in action, and I consider her the best in the business at what she does. She's known throughout the firm for being tough but fair. She shows a personal interest in each person who counts on her. And she does it all with no college degree or advanced education, but lots of good judgment and superb intuition. Here's one of the secrets to her success:

I've learned that to influence people over whom I have no authority, I have to communicate the same way that they do. When I communicate with consultants, they don't want to hear the details. They want answers. They also want to know why those answers benefit them, and that if they follow my suggestions, they won't have to worry about results. I achieve this by communicating my position clearly and with confidence so that they come to trust my expertise. The fact is, you're hired because others believe you're good at what you do. Actions and decisions applied consistently prove they were right. You have to see yourself as a partner in the process, not just a functionary who does exactly what she's told. I've got to be able to disagree if I think something won't work and provide reasons why, but I also have to recognize that in the end, I may not make the final decision. I've found that if I run my side of the business in a professional way and communicate in a way that other people can hear me, I'm able to influence others effectively.

Conversely, administrative professionals benefit greatly from knowing why they are being requested to do something or what particular decision has been made that probably affects them. It goes a long way to their acceptance and willingness if you give them the why.

Most of us find ourselves in many situations where, like Terry, we don't have the final say, and we have no formal authority or title to back us up. Her suggestion that we communicate in the same way the person we're trying to influence does is right on target. In addition to preparing our message in advance and saying it in an assertive manner, we've got to use words and language that others can relate to. Women actually know how to do this quite well. We've had years of practice as we've learned to influence our spouses, children, siblings, and parents. Think about how your tone of voice and word choice changes when you speak to each of these people. You just don't recognize when you're doing it.

VARYING YOUR INFLUENCE STYLE TO MEET THE NEEDS OF OTHERS

There's a model of influence I want to introduce you to that I've been teaching and using for years. It's pretty simple, and if you can get into the habit of using it when you're preparing to influence, you'll be more likely to achieve the outcomes you desire. Take a look at each of the following four shapes. See which one is most appealing to you. You'll probably be able to narrow it down to two pretty quickly, but choose just one in the end.

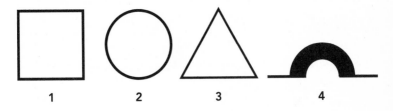

Each of the shapes represents a personality style that affects how we communicate. None of us is entirely one style or another—we possess elements of all four, but most people rely on one style to communicate more than the others. Knowing your style, and the style of others, can help you to effectively influence others by shaping your communications toward their preferences. The following chart describes what each of the shapes might mean:

USING COMMUNICATION STYLES TO INFLUENCE

Style	Wants to Know	How to Identify	How to Influence
1 The Reasoner	What are the facts?	Reasoners often dress conservatively, have offices that are somewhat spartan, and use language that reflects more concern for data than for human needs. They are sometimes described as cool, distant, or remote.	Avoid front-end small talk with Reasoners—they typically don't want to get too personal. They want "just the facts, ma'am." Prepare your communi-cations in advance by doing research and showing the logic in your proposal or idea.
2 The People Person	How do others feel about this idea?	People Persons will take the corporate uniform and personalize it with warm colors or accessories. Their offices may be filled with memorabilia from off-sites, family photos, and plants. They're quicker to say "I feel" than "I think," and will seek the opinions of others before making decisions.	Don't dive right in when approaching People Persons— take time to schmooze. Show that you've considered how your ideas will impact people or that you've gotten input from others. If your idea varies from how things have always been done, make a case for how it will actually make things better for others.

Style	Wants to Know	How to Identify	How to Influence
3 The Doer	What's the bottom line?	Doers dress comfortably and can be somewhat careless in their appearance (rolled-up sleeves, unpolished shoes, unpressed clothing). They speak quickly, using an economy of words, and their offices can look like a bomb went off. Dead plants are a dead giveaway.	Doers are fast thinkers who want the bottom line first. Be prepared with backup data, but don't review these unless asked—and even then, give an executive summary. Show that your proposal can be efficiently implemented and have a positive impact on the bottom line.
4 The Innovator	How will this idea position us for the future?	The Innovators are often wearing today what everyone else will be wearing tomorrow. Their offices frequently have toys, models, or abstract art. A check of their bookshelves will reveal an interest in trends and state-of-the-art thinking.	Being on the cutting edge matters to Innovators, so present your ideas in a manner that shows they're not simply a rehash of old thinking or old ways of doing things. Like Reasoners, Innovators like data, but not simply for data's sake. They use data to project or connect ideas.

As I said, we all possess characteristics of all four communication styles, so when determining the type of the person you're trying to influence you'll need to be observant and flexible. I once went out on a sales call, and—thinking that I was speaking with a Reasoner based on his office and how he was dressed—I began giving lots of data and a thorough explanation for why I thought his company could benefit from our training program. After a short time, I saw his foot start to tap. That was my cue that he was actually a Doer, so I quickly shifted to summarizing how the program would solve a particular problem he was having. It did the trick, and I walked away with his approval to move forward.

Some people have said they think using a model like this one—or many of the others that are out there—is manipulative. Nonsense. I liken it to being in a foreign country and trying to communicate with natives. If I can speak their language, I do. I don't change the actual content of my message—I change the manner in which I'm conveying it. It would be manipulative if I told people things I thought they wanted to hear rather than how I honestly saw the situation, but that's not what this is about. It's about framing the message so that other people can process it using *their* preferences—not mine.

If you're making a presentation to a large group where there will likely be many different preferences in the room, you can still use the model by ensuring there's something in it for everyone. Your presentation should contain elements that will appeal to as many people as possible by providing information, showing its impact on people, summarizing its efficiency, and explaining how it will position the company or organization for the future. Avoid the tendency to rely exclusively on *your* communication style in all situations.

Let me show you how this works by providing you with an example of the same idea presented to different personality types. Say you're a member of a nonprofit board that has been struggling with how to get more media coverage for the organization and raise more money for the cause. Before the next board meeting, you want to touch base with some of the more influential members to gather support for an idea you have. Here's what it would sound like when you communicate with each type of person:

- **With the Reasoner:** Ann, I'm calling because I want to explain to you an idea I'm going to be presenting at the next board meeting and get your support for it. I've done some research and found that 82 percent of organizations of our size hire media consultants to help them with their publicity campaigns. An investment of $100,000 for a consultant typically yields an increase of 60 percent in new donations in the $500 range, 20 percent more in donations from current contributors, and 15 percent less attrition in our donor base. In dollars and cents, that would mean we could potentially raise $750,000 annually on the initial $100,000 investment. What other *data* do you require to make a decision?

- **With the People Person:** Hi, Carl. Before I get down to business, I wanted to check to see how you're doing with the new job. I know transitions can be hard, and I'm wondering how yours is going. [Shift to listening.] Sounds like it's been a good move for you. I'm glad to hear it. Let me move on to why I called. I have an idea that I wanted to run by you to see if you would feel okay supporting me when I present it next week at the board meeting. I've checked around with some other boards of organizations of our size and found that people were pleasantly surprised by the results they got from using outside media consultants. Of course, choosing the right one for our organization will be important—we want someone who can line up behind our cause and communicate our values appropriately. People tell me when they find the right person, it can have a significant impact on getting the money needed to further the goals of our cause. They've found that an average investment of $100,000 can result in as much as $750,000 in additional annual contributions. I've spoken with a few other board members, and they feel it's something they can get behind. I'm wondering how you would *feel* about it?

- **With the Doer:** Jason, I know you're busy, and I don't want to take up too much of your time, so let me get to the point. At the next board meeting, I'm going to propose we hire an external consultant to handle our media campaign. Other organizations who have done this report that the bottom-line increase in additional contributions can be as much as 40 percent. That's not a bad return on investment. I've got all the data here that I would be happy to e-mail over to you if you'd like to see it. What else do you need to *move forward*?

- **With the Innovator:** Diana, as you know, we've been looking for ways to position our organization to be financially solid in the future and achieve our mission and financial goals. I've done some research with other organizations that needed to do the same and found that hiring an external media consultant can increase contributions by as much as

40 percent annually through attracting new donors, increasing contributions from existing donors, and reducing attrition from our current donor base. Four of the ten people I surveyed said they were worried about having to close their doors in eighteen months, but the consultant really turned that around for them. Since our primary concern is ensuring fiscal viability for the next three to five years, I believe this alternative will fit in nicely with our strategic plan. How can we *position this idea* with the board to gain buy-in that will *secure our future*?

VARYING YOUR INFLUENCE STYLE TO SUIT THE SITUATION

There's one more factor to consider when devising your strategy for influencing others: the situation. If you think about it, there are times when you are the expert about a particular subject, and people will be influenced by this. But there are many other situations to think about. Perhaps you want to be more insistent on going in the direction you suggest because you have legitimate concerns or the right to do so; maybe you want to convince people that a novel idea is the way to go but you have no real facts to support the direction; or perhaps outcomes are less important in a particular case than maintaining relationships. Each of these situations requires a different influence tactic, and assessing in advance which style would be most appropriate will increase the likelihood of achieving your desired outcomes. The following are five tactics to consider and the best time to use them:

- **Facts:** The use of facts and figures to influence others to go in a particular direction is most effective when you are a *subject-matter expert* or when you have all the information needed to influence people to make a data-driven decision. Here's an example of influencing through the use of facts: "The research shows that only 20 percent of the income of organizations of our size and nature is from Internet sales. On the other hand, 60 percent of their income is derived from media advertising. This makes it clear that we should be putting more of our resources into the latter approach."

- **Declarations:** There are times when your legitimate needs, wants, or expectations will take precedence over just the facts. This is when you would use a declarative statement to influence. Be aware that declarations can damage relationships, which is why you want to use them sparingly and only in emergencies, situations in which you have exhausted other alternatives and your formal or informal authority supports the declaration, or where you are willing to forgo the relationship for achieving the desired outcome. For example, suppose you have a follower reporting to you who is underperforming, and you have already used the available data to show him the number of mistakes he's making, the number of days he's come to work late, or the number of projects he's working on that aren't meeting your expectations. Given that there has been no change in performance, you might then shift to using a declaration as an influence tactic. The key here is that you state your expectations clearly followed by consequences. It sounds like this: "We've talked before about the fact that your performance is not meeting departmental standards. I want to make it clear that if you do not increase the number of projects you deliver on time and error-free, your employment with the company will be in jeopardy." As you can hear, this is more direct and deliberate approach than simply providing the facts and letting people come to a logical conclusion.

- **Connectors:** Using connectors to influence is effective when there are differences of opinion as to a particular decision or direction and it's important to maintain open communication and relationships. The tactic entails openly listening to the ideas of others, restating your understanding of them, and looking for ways to tie your thoughts together with or build on those of others. In my experience, women tend to over-rely on connectors to the exclusion of developing the other four influence skills. Here's an example of influencing through connectors: "If I heard you correctly, you believe that we should not take action on this until we have gathered more information. Although I agree that additional information will be helpful and that we should do more research, I also believe we need to begin to move forward with the data we already have or we will miss out on this window of opportunity." You can hear that this is a much more conciliatory approach to influencing than the first two.

- **Emotional appeals:** When novel or unique ideas are presented, it can be difficult for others, particularly those who tend to be concrete or unimaginative, to actually envision what the idea would look like in reality. People who use emotional appeals choose vivid words and paint a verbal picture that will excite, inspire, and motivate others to go in the suggested direction. As such, the tactic requires a fundamental understanding of the audience's needs or interests. Otherwise, an emotional appeal can sound like a harebrained scheme. It sounds similar to this: "You've talked about the need for a product that will propel our organization to the next level, excite our customers, and motivate our sales staff to reach monthly goals like never before. Well, I've got just such a product. I want you to picture yourself sitting in your living room after a hard day's work and being massaged by the most powerful and effective therapeutic chair ever manufactured. It's like having thirty tiny fingers working the stress out of your neck and back. Unlike other products, this one can be customized to meet the decor needs of the buyer and contains a motor that is guaranteed for ten years. There's nothing like it on the market today, and we have an opportunity to be the exclusive distributor of this newly designed product."

- **Detaching:** Most people don't think of detaching from a discussion or not even bringing an idea up in the first place as a form of influence, but it is. The ability to read a situation and know when to hold 'em or fold 'em is an influence skill many people would do well to learn. Let's say you've introduced the suggestion at a community meeting that one of the town officials be removed from her post. You've provided a good rationale and didn't expect it to be met with so much controversy. The meeting erupts in chaos, with people stubbornly taking sides, name calling, and much bitterness. It's clear that the group will not be able to make a decision at this meeting. Detaching is the smartest thing to do at the moment. A comment such as "I can see that this suggestion is going to require a lot more discussion and perhaps even more research. I move to table it until our next meeting" would be appropriate for the situation and give you more time to develop a broader rationale or the alliances you need to be able to influence the group. Similarly, let's say you want a raise. Then the company's last-quarter earnings are announced, and they're below expectations. The timing just isn't right to bring up the subject, so you decide to hold off for a few weeks. Relinquishing the need to ask for the raise right now (or detaching from the idea) is a smart influence move because it will increase the likelihood of getting a raise at a later time.

Hopefully, this chapter has caused you to think about the many factors that go into being able to successfully influence others. What's most important is that you *consciously* prepare your influence communications in advance, using *all* of the strategies suggested for becoming a more effective influencer.

Coaching Tips for Influencing

27. **Be clear on the front end what you want on the back end.** There's an old Chinese curse that runs, *May you have a wonderful idea and not be able to convince anyone of it.* You're more likely to suffer from this curse if you don't know what you want the outcomes to be *before* you start to influence. Whether from fear of rejection or of being called names, women are less likely than men to express exactly what they want, when they want it, and how they want to go about achieving it. The result? They get less. If you're going in to ask for a raise, be clear about how much you want. If you're proposing an idea, be clear about what it is and how it can be achieved.

28. ***Be assertive.*** Strong leaders exhibit a willingness to say things that are difficult to say—and others may find difficult to hear—but that must be said. To do otherwise can be construed as colluding with a status quo that does the organization no good. Keep in mind that assertiveness means you combine direct and clear communication with unfailing, unconditional positive regard and concern for others. If you've been passive in the past, you might confuse assertiveness with aggressiveness and go overboard.

29. ***Avoid the tendency to go from one extreme of the assertiveness continuum to the other.*** When women are assertive and then get shot down, they often have the tendency to shift to being more passive. Resist the tendency to acquiesce in the face of disagreement—it doesn't mean you're wrong, only that the other person has a different, perhaps equally legitimate viewpoint.

30. ***Know your audience.*** What's important to them? How will your idea help them solve a problem? What do you have to give in exchange for what you want? Having a good idea isn't enough—it has to be valuable to the people you're trying to sell it to. Couch your influencing communications in ways that show you understand the needs of the other person and have identified ways to meet those needs.

31. ***Look for points of agreement.*** This means finding ways to bridge your ideas with those of others. Listen carefully to others and pinpoint places where their concepts overlap with yours. Beginning your statements with a point of agreement makes even new or differing suggestions seem less confrontational.

32. ***Get to the point.*** Women have the tendency to use far more words than needed when influencing. They think that if they

talk enough, their points will become crystal clear—when in fact the opposite is true. Begin your communications with the one statement you would want others to remember if you had only enough time to say that.

33. ***Vary your influence style.*** Most of us tend to rely on one influence style that we're comfortable with—even though it doesn't always work. The best influencers don't communicate in ways *they're* comfortable with—they position their ideas in ways others can best hear. If you tend to make emotional pleas for support, shift to providing more data. If you're inclined to come up with novel ideas, accompany them with practical execution strategies. Be more strategic in preparing to influence.

34. ***Combine declarative statements with inclusive taglines.*** Unlike men, women have to walk the fine line between sounding self-confident and exhibiting concern for what others think. This doesn't mean they're expected to change their positions without good reason, but they are expected to be open to alternative viewpoints. By combining a strong statement of opinion with a tagline that invites the opinions of others, you can avoid being called the feared B-word.

35. ***Act "as if."*** When I was a little girl and there was something I was afraid to do, my mother used to tell me to sing the song "I Whistle a Happy Tune" from *The King and I*. In essence, she was telling me to act *as if* I was confident, and everything would turn out okay—and it usually did. Of course you're not going to go around whistling in an effort to muster up the courage to influence others, but you *can* act with confidence regardless of how you're feeling inside.

36. ***Be strategic about your influence communications.*** Even if you're the most articulate person in the world, it's still impor-

tant to plan in advance for achieving your desired outcomes. You can do this by mentally rehearsing or writing down an outline of the key points you want to cover, the influence style you're going to use to deliver them, and the type of person you're attempting to influence. Remember: *Chance favors the prepared mind.*

37. ***Capitalize on your passion and values.*** Women are fortunate in that they have social permission to use a wide range of emotions in their communications; men aren't always accorded that latitude. It may not be appropriate to be your most effusive self in an important meeting, but showing that you have strong feelings about a topic can reflect your commitment to outcomes. Also, using a wide range (not the *full* range) of your emotions rather than stifling them can let people know when you're in full agreement with a particular issue.

38. ***Volunteer to make formal and informal presentations.*** People often tell me I'm a great public speaker. I'm always honored and flattered by the feedback, but the fact is that practice makes perfect—or a close approximation. From the time I was president of my high school junior and senior classes, I've been in front of a microphone. When circumstances keep me from speaking for any length of time, I'm as anxious as the next person when I have to walk up to the podium and begin a presentation. If you want to become really good at influencing others, seize every opportunity to go outside your comfort zone and speak before large and small groups.

CHAPTER FIVE

From Cheerleader to Coach: Motivating People to Achieve Their Best

You take people as far as they will go—not as far as you would like them to go.
> —Jeannette Rankin, first woman elected to Congress

You've already coached others if you've:

- Taught a child to ride a bike.
- Showed a new coworker the ropes.
- Encouraged a friend, spouse, or partner to make a career move.
- Coached a pregnant woman through childbirth.
- Trained someone in an area of your expertise.

Behind every great man, there's a great woman—or so the saying goes. Where would Clyde be without Bonnie? Franklin without Eleanor? George without Gracie? Fred without Ginger? Bill without Hillary? If there's one thing a woman knows, it's how to be a cheerleader for others. Whether it's with spouses, best friends, or children, we are the quintessential cheerleaders, helpmates, sounding boards, and fans. At times we're far better at motivating others than we are at motivating ourselves. But let's save that for another book. The point is, throughout history women have coached others to achieve great things—but we didn't call it coaching.

Perhaps one of the greatest business coaches of all time was Mary Kay Ash, founder of Mary Kay Cosmetics. Her ability to motivate, excite, and instill passion in others contributed to not only her own success but also that of millions of other women around the globe. Mary Kay passed away in 2001, so it wasn't possible to interview her for this book, but I was fortunate enough to be able to speak with three women who worked closely with her:

- Nancy Thomason, currently executive project specialist, traveled with Mary Kay as head of her protection detail and has been with the company for twenty-five years.

- Jennifer Cook, museum director, started as a clerk with the company in 1971, later became Mary Kay's secretary, and eventually managed her administrative staff. She's been with the company for thirty-five years.

- Yvonne Pendleton worked directly with Mary Kay on communications projects. She has been with Mary Kay, Inc., for fourteen years and is director of corporate communication and corporate heritage.

I began my interview with these women by asking what made Mary Kay so inspiring to them personally and how she impacted their lives. What followed was a lively and inspiring conversation about a woman who not only founded a billion-dollar business but also changed the lives of women along the way. Here's some of what they shared:

Jennifer: Mary Kay was the most gracious person I've ever met. She used to tell me, "Pretend people have a sign around their necks that says MAKE ME FEEL IMPORTANT." She didn't just shake hands with you, she took your hand and grasped it in her two hands, then looked you in the eye and really listened. She never took her eyes off you when she was talking to you. She had an amazing ability to block off all distractions.

Nancy: It was my job to get her from one appointment to another on time, and it was hard to get her attention if she was talking to someone. It was not the most enviable position to be in to interrupt a conversation Mary Kay was engaged in to advise her that she had another appointment and had to leave. She would never break off the conversation herself. Everyone admired her so much and wanted to talk to her, but she was always humble. If she went into a reception, everyone was important. She would talk to the waiters—not migrate to the most important person in the room. Once when we were in Washington, DC, for a meeting, Mary Kay turned down an invitation to the White House because she already had a commitment to fly back to Dallas for a meeting with new employees at the company.

Jennifer: People were important to her. She got involved in their lives and made you feel like a partner in building this great organization. I raised three children working for Mary Kay. Because she was a mother herself, she knew which priorities were important. One time I got a call from my daughter's day care school. She had gotten into some medicine, and I was so shocked, I was just sitting there. Mary Kay said, "You've got to leave *now*. Put down what you're doing." At those times, she was right there for you.

Nancy: If she knew anyone in our independent sales force was in the hospital, she would call them. If someone had to have surgery, the first call they received afterward was from Mary Kay. If they lived out of state and she found out they didn't have the right medical attention, she would arrange for them to have a consultation in Dallas. She connected with everyone. Sometimes blind sales force members would communicate with her by audiotapes. I would wonder to myself, *Who thinks she's going to listen to an hour-long tape?* But she did.

Nancy: Mary Kay walked the talk. She did everything she ever asked the sales force to do. Once she challenged the sales force to have a ten-show week and decided she would join the challenge. She started calling people to have a skin care class and wound up booking twenty.

Yvonne: She'd been practicing her beliefs for a long time before her theories became standard in business. When she wrote about her leadership philosophy in the 1980s, everyone thought it was so novel, and she wondered, "Isn't that the way everyone runs their business?" She didn't do these things because some business guru said to do it; she saw this as the way to do business long before everyone else was talking about it. One of Mary Kay's greatest strengths was her ability to believe in people a long time before they believed in themselves. She instilled this ability in our sales force leaders, too. She said one of the greatest strengths of a leader was in helping people believe in themselves.

Nancy: She knew recognition and praise were powerful motivators. Women often work harder for recognition and praise than for money.

Jennifer: She taught women to set goals. Your life shouldn't just happen—you need to make those things happen.

Yvonne: Mary Kay always challenged herself to do better and reach higher goals.

Nancy: You never rest on your laurels. You always raise the bar.

Jennifer: She developed a whole company of leaders.

Yvonne: And our leaders in the independent sales force know it's their responsibility to create new leaders—to bring someone along with you. That's how a worldwide sales force of 1.3 million happened. She came along with her dream company and her opportunity for women at a time when no one was encouraging women to do anything. There was no career path for women other than in nursing or teaching, and she realized she could bring several generations of women to levels of achievement they had never before dared to imagine.

Jennifer: She had a great personal charisma. When people met her, it was like a landmark meeting. Even people who left the company under not pleasant circumstances might have been mad at their supervisor, but they still loved Mary Kay.

Yvonne: The bottom line is, all these years later her principles still work. Every day we follow the principles she started this company with. This morning, I was talking to one of our new hires who had been hugely successful at other big companies. She said, "I've only been here four weeks and feel this is the place I want to stay and make a difference."

Jennifer: Mary Kay was consistent. She never wavered when she thought something was right. If she knew it was the right thing to do, she did it. It wasn't that she was against change—she knew you had to change to remain successful—but the most fundamental principles—such as treating people by the golden rule, living your priorities, acting with integrity, and making people feel important—she wouldn't waver on. She believed *P&L* means "people and love" as well as "profit and loss."

Yvonne: She turned the phrase *People are known by the company they keep* into *A company is really known by the people that it keeps.* She valued every person no matter what their position and knew they were critical to the success of our company—and that's how she referred to it, as *our* company. She corrected me one day when I called it *your* company.

Lois: The story goes when she started her business, people told her she couldn't possibly be successful. How did she deal with that?

Jennifer: That's true. It was 1963, and her attorney sent her a pamphlet on how many cosmetics companies go broke every year. Her accountant told her she'd go broke with the commission schedule she set. She said she wasn't in it to make a lot of money, she was in it to give women an opportunity.

Nancy: She started the company with her savings of five thousand dollars. Her husband was going to be the administrator, and the week before they were to open the doors her husband died at the breakfast table. So she called her family together and asked what she should do. They encouraged her to go ahead.

Lois: What experience did she have that made her think she could be successful?

Jennifer: As a single mom, she worked in direct sales first for Stanley Home Products, then later for a company called World Gift. She knew that with three kids at home, direct sales was the only kind of job that would allow her to have balance between her work and her family.

Nancy: She used to say she knew what it was like to hit the glass ceiling, and she wanted to start a company that would remove the obstacles for women. When she worked at World Gift, she would come up with all these ideas and would be told, "You're thinking like a woman, Mary Kay." After she left and was so successful, her old boss called her up one day and asked how she did it. She told him, "I told you how to do it, but you didn't listen to me!" It would have paid to listen to her.

Jennifer: She grew up really poor. Her father was an invalid, and her mother worked in a restaurant. A lot of the communication she had with her mother was over the phone; Mary Kay would call her at work and ask her what to do about one thing or another. Her mother would always encourage her and tell her, "You can do it, Mary Kay." This became the model for her entire life—knowing she could do what she put her mind to.

Lois: As I'm listening to you, I'm becoming inspired! How did she instill such inspiration in others?

Yvonne: Mary Kay had this ageless ability to understand what motivated women of all ages and backgrounds. She was truly one of the great communicators. Her messages were always on point, and they always left people with a takeaway. We still integrate her messages into our meetings. We talk about and practice her principles and her leadership. She never forgot where she came from. It was never about *Look at me,* it was about *This is what it takes and this is what works for me,* but then she also knew everyone had to do it their own way. As a wife and mother, I think the message I most appreciated from Mary Kay was that setting your priorities is so important to achieving balance in your life. And she always gave us so many examples of women who lived by her creed of God first, family second, career third.

Jennifer: She'd tell you to hitch your wagon to a star. When she first started out, she hitched her wagon to the Queen of Sales in Stanley Home Products.

Yvonne: She also believed you should tell someone what you're going to do. She marched up to the VP of the company and told him, "Next year I'm going to be the Queen of Sales." If you tell someone who's supportive of you that you're going to do it, then you have to do it. She constantly challenged herself, and as the company was growing she challenged her leaders in the same way.

Lois: Did she ever sit back, look around her, and say, *Wow, look at what I've accomplished?*

Yvonne: Far from that. Mary Kay was one of the most humble, down-to-earth people you'd ever meet.

Jennifer: All she talked about was the success of others. A good day for her was when she learned one more woman was able to step out of her comfort zone and believe in herself. When she went to Germany, what excited her the most was that the German Mary Kay business consultants were experiencing the same growth as here in the US. When the Berlin Wall came down, she was in Germany, and someone said, "First we get freedom, then we get Mary Kay!" Mary Kay loved it. That's what she remembered. If people talked about *your* company, she talked about *our* company. It's the shared vision of everyone involved. She felt every person was important in building it.

I believe being a *woman* is precisely what enabled Mary Kay to break the conventional rules about success in business. Mary Kay exemplified the leadership behaviors contained in every chapter of this book, but the success of her company was contingent upon ensuring the success of those around her and doing it in a way that met *their* needs, not hers. And that is the essence of great coaching.

COACHING: A FEMININE PERSPECTIVE

To get a feminine perspective on coaching, my colleague Dr. Karen Otazo and I surveyed women sports coaches. One of the few sports where women achieve international recognition equal to that of male sports figures is tennis—and that's largely due to the efforts of Billie Jean King. To find out what women coaches think are the keys to bringing out the best in players, we spoke with two successful tennis coaches: Julie Anthony and Jane Albert Willens. They each spoke of the importance of building trusting relationships where players can hear and incorporate feedback. In addition, they each spoke of the need to understand and work with a player's mental and performance anxiety.

Jane Albert Willens, a Wimbledon contender, a tennis coach, and the daughter of Frankie Albert (former left-handed quarterback for the San Francisco 49ers), told us that successful coaching is about "building self-esteem by focusing on strengths. People are resistant to change because of the risk it involves. You build self-esteem by letting them know what they're doing right—then they're more willing to take risks." She explained that even good coaches have the tendency to write people off if they don't "get it right" the first time—but getting past player fears is critical if you want to help them, and you, to succeed.

Coach Willens provided a beautiful example of encouraging incremental change. She explained how difficult it can be to get a player to change from a forehand to a service grip. While the former is more comfortable and natural, the latter yields better results. Willens has players rotate the racket only infinitesimally during each practice drill until eventually it's in the service grip position. She also knows that fear of failure often causes people to look as if they actually *want* to fail. Patience with the mistakes players make and the willingness to provide constant feedback to correct those mistakes are her keys to success.

Julie Anthony, who coached world number one doubles player and Olympic gold medalist Gigi Fernandez, echoed Willens's remarks, adding, "Successful coaching involves understanding the pressure and anxiety players are under. Getting inside players' heads. They're prisoners of their own minds." When asked what she would tell leaders who want to know how to do this, she responded, "By listening, not talking. Hearing about [players'] experience and not telling them what you think you saw. It's a mistake to start talking to them when they come off the court. That's the time to listen." Is coaching people in the game of tennis any different from coaching people to be successful in the boardroom? "Tennis is like anything else in life when you have to perform for someone else," Anthony said. "Some just perform more publicly than others. Players must trust coaches so much that they can surrender to the process—be willing to experience the prerequisite discomfort that accompanies change."

Trust, caring, inspiring, teaching—all important themes for learning how to be a peak performer on the playing field of sports and life. Leaders can learn important lessons from their coaching colleagues. In the last chapter, I introduced Terry Monahan of

McKinsey & Company, and described how she influences people over whom she has little or no authority. She may not be a sports coach, but she does have to motivate a staff in a professional service firm that is notorious for its exceedingly high expectations, where the flat nature of the firm leaves little room for upward mobility, and doing the impossible is de rigueur. Although I've known her for nearly twenty years, I'd never asked what makes her a master motivator. When I did, I was surprised at how closely aligned our philosophies are:

> *I'm not a leader if no one wants to follow me. It comes down to getting my staff to first trust me. The way I do that is to make time for them when they need me—not when I have time for them. You can't just pay lip service to people when it comes to caring about them. You have to come across in a way that shows genuine concern for the person, not just the problems they face. I care as much about how they feel when they leave the room as I do about helping them to solve their problems. A lot of leaders are afraid if they let that compassionate, human side show, they'll be taken advantage of. I haven't found that to be true. For me, showing that I care and getting their trust includes three important people skills: accepting that people are different and need different things from me; not guessing what motivates someone but asking them and getting them to say it; and making it a point to know what was going on with them not just by walking around saying good morning, but by writing down what they tell me is happening so they know—and I know—it will be remembered.*

What Terry shares is fundamental to being a good coach and motivator. I've always believed it's not that hard to get people to do what you want if you use enough muscle. What results, however, is subversive compliance—people who do exactly what you ask and nothing more or different, even when the situation calls for it. Good leaders don't aim for *compliance;* they aim for *commitment.* Committed people will go the extra mile, support decisions made by the leader, and act in the best interests of the organization even when no one is watching over them. And the way to get that commitment begins with the individual relationships you build with those upon whom you depend to get the job done—whether that job is in a corporation, on a volunteer committee, or in a nonprofit organization.

BUILDING RELATIONSHIPS WITH FOLLOWERS

You may recall the line that came out of the Bill Clinton camp when he ran against George Bush for president: *It's the economy, stupid.* Well, I've always wanted to write a leadership book titled *It's the Relationship, Stupid,* but the "nice girl" in me wouldn't take it the next step. The fact is, coaching success is all in the relationship—and that's yet another place where women excel. The problem is, we're *so* good at it that we often confuse our leadership responsibilities with a desire to maintain those relationships *at all costs.* The leader-follower relationship is similar in several important aspects to the relationships you have with the people you most trust in your own life. Think about it. You trust people who are honest with you, who are willing to tell you things you may not *want* to hear but that you *need* to hear, and who you know have your best interests at heart. Trust comes from their loyalty to you, from their support, and from their genuine concern for you as a human being. The same holds true for leaders and followers. Building relationships in which you have the latitude to say tough things and ask for the impossible is key to your role as a coach and motivator. Where it stops, however, is in the expectation that your followers will do the same for you. That's not the quid pro quo in the leader-follower relationship. Followers don't have the responsibility to support, be loyal to, and show a genuine concern for you—those are by-products of having successfully built a trusting relationship, and the responsibility to do that is *yours*, not *theirs*. As the philosopher Lao-tzu said, "Fail to honor people, they fail to honor you."

I was once discussing this concept with the participants in a leadership workshop I was facilitating. One man who had been particularly quiet throughout the program told the group this story that I never forgot because it so eloquently expresses the importance of building trust in the leader-follower relationship:

As the manager of the maintenance department at a large oil refinery, I had a team of pretty tough union guys. There was one guy in particular who would ignore me every day when I walked by and said good morning. One day I noticed that he looked kind of dejected. I called him into my office and asked if anything was wrong. He told me that he was preoccupied with his wife's health; she was recently diagnosed with cancer and had begun chemotherapy treatments. He was quite emotional at points, and I just listened, not knowing quite what to say. The longer he went on, the more concerned I was that I was wasting the company's money by having him there in my office for nearly an hour; but I just let him talk. When he finished, I asked him if there was anything I could do. He said not really, but thanks for offering. Before he left, I said I wanted to ask him a question. Why did he ignore me each day when I walked by and said good morning?

He seemed puzzled, then asked me which side I walked by. I told him it was usually his left side. He smiled and said he was deaf in that ear. We laughed together and I felt something had shifted between us.

Then a few days later he came into my office for the first time without me asking him to. He said that there was a particular piece of machinery that looked as if it was about to break down. I knew that if it did, it could cost thousands of dollars in production time. He said if I would authorize him to buy a particular part, he could fix it before the problem got any worse. Of course I gave him the go-ahead, but it taught me a good lesson about the importance of taking the time to see employees as human beings, not just union workers. Here I was worrying about spending an hour of the company's money and he saved us thousands of dollars.

That man's story taught everyone in the class a more valuable lesson than I could have conveyed with all the textbook examples in the world. The time he took to show an interest in one of his staff members paid dividends that he could never have imagined. And that's the beauty of building relationships—when you need a relationship, it's already too late to build it. You can't coach people you're not in a relationship with. If you try, it will simply look like an attempt to get more work out of them, and they'll resist the efforts of even the best coaches. It's what makes it imperative that you constantly and consistently take time to build strong relationships with those upon whom you depend. Here's a checklist of things you can do to build relationships:

- **Have doorway conversations:** When you're walking down the hall, stop by people's offices and engage in casual conversation while standing in the doorway. Ask about the person's family; if you know she's a movie buff, ask if she's seen any good ones lately; ask a gourmand for suggestions for new restaurants. Keep it casual and short.

- **Learn about people's aspirations:** When walking to the parking garage or over lunch, ask people what they've done that they're most proud of or what they hope to achieve.

- **Invite one new person each week to lunch:** Here, too, keep the conversation casual and strive to get to know the person on a personal, not just work, level. Be prepared to open the kimono a little to let yourself show as well. By this I mean: Don't be afraid to talk about things that are personally meaningful to you. For example, share your frustration with the inadequate care a nursing home is providing to an elderly parent, or your delight with that fact that your son was accepted into his college of choice. Just be sure to avoid deep dark secrets—no one needs to hear about your dirty laundry.

- **Ask for input in an area of someone's expertise:** If you're about to buy a new car and you know you've got an automobile aficionado on your staff, ask for advice or sources of information.

- **Join in on after-hours events:** This can be a little tough for women, given how much we often have to do after work, but making the extra effort to orchestrate it is worth it. You don't have to stay long, but making an effort to socialize with others can humanize you to them—and them to you. Take care not to drink too much or say things you'll regret in the morning.

- **Notice and comment on behavioral changes:** If people just don't seem like themselves, ask if anything's wrong. Even if they say no, they'll appreciate your concern.

- **Be human:** Too many leaders think they have an image to uphold. They don't realize it's not the image they should be concerned about, but letting others see them as a human being. You're not a role, you're a person—act like one.

Building relationships with followers doesn't have to lead to what Mom warned you about: *Familiarity breeds contempt.* It's more like what football legend Knute Rockne said when asked his secret of successful coaching: "Strict discipline combined with kindly interest in the boys." Here again, afraid that they may damage a relationship, women are often fearful of expressing their expectations clearly, then holding people accountable for goal achievement. Which brings us to the next pre-coaching consideration: letting people know what's expected of them.

WHAT ARE THE EXPECTATIONS?

Believe it or not, most people don't want to make your life miserable. It may sometimes *seem* that way, but it's almost always the result of poorly communicated expectations or misunderstandings around mutual needs. I believe that *if people knew better, they'd do better*. There's a great book called *The Set-Up-to-Fail Syndrome: How Good Managers Cause Great People to Fail* by Jean-François Manzoni and Jean-Louis Barsoux. As the title suggests, the authors talk about the ways in which leaders' misperceptions, the labels they place on others, and their own blind spots get in the way of bringing out the best in their followers. Good coaches avoid this by defining and articulating their expectations for excellence.

They don't do this simply during a yearly performance review, but rather at every opportunity.

I recently gave a keynote address about leadership to the senior staff of Sony Pictures Television. Before the program began, I asked one of the organizers who she considered to be one of their best female leaders. She told me it was a woman by the name of Flory Bramnick, senior vice president for West Coast sales and cable distribution. Fortunately for me, Flory attended the keynote. Observing her before, during, and after my presentation, I could see why she was considered a good leader. She was poised and self-confident yet humble and unassuming. When I asked if I could interview her and she consented, I was delighted. I wanted to know why she thought others considered her a good leader. Here's what she said:

> To be an effective leader, a woman must stop thinking about the fact that she's a woman. I say that because leadership is about bringing people together, not about creating distinctions. It's about others, not about you. As soon as you become self-conscious, you're likely to go over a cliff. Similarly, you don't graduate to leadership. You learn it every day. You learn it's not about being the smartest person in the room or having the right answer; it's about having a goal that's so clear to you and that you're so personally excited about that people want to engage with you. This is where your values, goals, and actions have to be aligned. Once you get that, you can get down to the business of hearing other people, what their needs are, and truly motivating them. Although you can lead by virtue of your position and get people to do what you want, you've got to be concerned with how they feel about the direction in which you're taking them and

whether it's consistent with their needs, too. My job as a leader is
to get commitment to the goal based on what I try to ensure are
mutually shared values. Anything short of that is unacceptable.

Flory makes a number of great points about leadership and
motivation that I want to underscore:

- It's about others, not about you.
- Your values, goals, and actions have to be aligned.
- You have to be excited about what you're doing if you want
  others to be.
- It's critical to find ways to ensure that the needs of others are
  being met if you want them to fully commit to the direction
  in which you're moving.
- You can't accept less than full commitment to the organization's goals.

In essence, she's saying that inspiration is caught, not taught.
It's pretty tough to coach someone if *you're* not excited about the
direction in which you're moving. She also says something that
many leaders don't want to openly admit—if you've got players who
aren't lined up behind the goals you establish, they don't belong
on the team. In this case, your coaching should shift to developing
exit strategies so they can find something more suitable for them.
I'll be talking about how to do that a little later in this chapter.

My experience is that people typically don't need coaching
in their areas of technical competence. If that were the case, you
would send them for technical training, not coach them. Most
people derail because they fail to exhibit one or more of the
norms expected within their organizational culture. That is, in

every organization there are norms for success. Some of these include:

- Be a team player.
- Act ethically.
- Communicate openly.
- Take risks.
- Be frugal.
- Compete aggressively.
- Be flexible.
- Collaborate on major projects.
- Go the extra mile.
- Be friendly and collegial.
- Plan and organize work effectively.

What are the standards for success that *you* employ? Write them down. Talk to people about them. Explain how they will be measured against them. This requires being able to take those standards and translate them into *observable* behaviors. For example, what would it look like to you if someone was acting like a team player? A trick I use when coaching clients is to pretend I have a video camera trained on them as they go through their workday. If they were behaving consistently with their leader's expectations, what would it capture? The camera can't see "team player," but it can see people finishing their work, then offering to help others; fully participating in team discussions even when they're not about their own area of expertise; or circulating articles of mutual interest to coworkers. These are specific and measurable behaviors that you can use to articulate your expectations.

The effective coach puts herself in the shoes of players who aren't performing up to expectations and assumes they don't *know* what to do differently. Women are good at assuming they've done something wrong; here's a place where it will really come in handy. I tell all my clients—male and female—that the first place to look when they're dealing with someone who isn't achieving goals is at *themselves*. How have you failed to be clear about the goals, expectations, or standards of measurement? Once you answer this question and take action on it, you can shift to addressing the development areas of others.

THE 7:1 RULE OF COACHING

So far I've talked about building relationships and clearly telling people how you plan to hold them accountable. But do you catch people in the act of doing things right and reinforce those behaviors? The 7:1 Rule says that you have to give people seven pieces of positive feedback for every one piece of developmental feedback—and not all at the same time. In other words, you can't say, *I like how you did this, this, and this, and by the way, you've got to change this other thing over here.* Positive feedback has to be given as close as possible to the event or behavior you're reinforcing. There are also three stipulations: It must be genuine, specific, and free from implied criticism. While the first two caveats are self-explanatory, people often ask what's meant by *implied criticism*. When I asked if anyone in a class of twenty-five people could explain what it meant, a woman participant responded quite eloquently: "It's like when my mother-in-law comes for dinner and says, 'This soup is delicious. You finally learned how to cook!'" The first part of the message would be great by itself, but it's eclipsed by the second part, which implies that she didn't know how to cook before.

I remember talking to a client about the 7:1 Rule and having her tell me she had a hard time complimenting people for doing what they're *supposed* to do. I asked her, "Does the praise come out of your paycheck or benefits?" Of course not. That's why I can never understand why so many leaders are so reluctant to give well-earned praise when positive reinforcement increases the likelihood of the desired behavior being repeated in the future. Let me give you an illustration of how it works. Let's say you're in Las Vegas playing the slot machines. You put a quarter into the machine—and what happens? If you have luck like mine, most likely nothing happens. You put in another quarter, and again, nothing comes back. But after several more tries, you get back a few coins. That's positive reinforcement at work! The little amount of money that's returned to you keeps you feeding the machine *more* money because you think you're eventually going to hit the jackpot. Psychologists call this *intermittent positive reinforcement.* When employed consistently, it serves to significantly increase the likelihood that the behavior you're reinforcing will continue.

One workplace study asked managers what they thought motivated their people most; the response was "Money." The same study asked employees what motivated them most. Their reply? "Appreciation." Some leaders think this means they have to hand-hold and coddle followers. Not true. A kind word or note after a particularly good job, or upon successful completion of a requested behavioral change, will assure a repeat performance of that behavior. The employee will, consciously or otherwise, go for the "quarter"—in this case, the praise. We're talking about five minutes of your time that can pay off big rewards in the long term. Showing appreciation for the work of your employees needn't be time consuming or even an everyday occurrence with the same person. If it is, followers wind up feeling the appreciation is meaningless or not genuine.

It's all too easy to unintentionally reinforce the wrong behavior if you're not specific about what you'd like to see continued. That happened to me when I was working full time and going to school to complete my doctorate at night. I would come to work each morning and spend an hour or so writing my dissertation. When performance review time came, my boss rated me "outstanding" and told me what a fine job I was doing, but he didn't mention anything specific. He unknowingly reinforced my behavior.

You might tell an employee, "You did a great job on the Adler account," but the employee may not know which part you were particularly pleased with. In fact, the employee may have screwed up one part that you didn't know about—and now you've inadvertently reinforced the mistake! Or you could say, "You did a fine job on the analysis of the P&L on the Adler account . . . it was a lot better than the analysis of the Konig account." The problem here is that the implied criticism obscures the message. The best message is one that is direct, clear, and clean: "Steve, you did a great job with developing the five-year plan on the Robinson account. The clients expressed a great deal of satisfaction with its specificity, and I was impressed with the research you did to make it so robust." Don't let your followers say about you what we often hear them saying about other leaders: "No news is good news."

The bottom line is: You want people to do what's expected of them—and to continue doing it indefinitely. Intermittent positive reinforcement ensures that it will. It costs you nothing but can pay huge dividends. It also lets followers know that you notice what they're doing right—not only what they're doing wrong. By giving seven pieces of positive feedback for each piece of developmental feedback, you reduce the likelihood that the person will see you as overly critical. When I ask managers what ratio they use for feedback, they usually laugh and say it's quite the opposite! My own observation is that women have a much less difficult time with this than do men. Women intuitively know how positive reinforcement works and use it to their advantage.

COACHING IN BOUNDS

Now—and only now—you're ready to coach. You've taken the time to build the relationship. You've been clear about your expectations. People don't see you as overly critical because you give seven times more positive reinforcement than negative. And in the model I'm about to explain, you're not going to focus on the negative, which makes it ideal for women. We tend to be more sensitive than men to criticism, which is probably why we don't criticize as often as we could—or should. That's going to serve you well in this coaching model I've developed. I don't believe criticism serves to shape desired behavior. You know it doesn't work with your children or spouse, so why would criticism work with your followers? Instead, this model neutralizes feedback so that people can hear it, yet it will be direct and honest—and that's something many women need to learn!

If you read my book *Nice Girls Don't Get the Corner Office*, then you know I believe the workplace is a playing field. It has boundaries, rules, and strategies that all must be respected to win the game. Feedback is about getting people who are currently out of bounds back in. It's not that they're doing something *wrong*—it's that they're not doing *enough* of something, or they're doing *too much* of it. Look at the following table. It describes how you might begin to prepare for a coaching session with someone who is not meeting your expectations.

DEVELOPMENTAL PLAYING FIELD:
ORGANIZATION AND PLANNING

Out of Bounds (Doing Too Much)	In Bounds (Do More)	Out of Bounds (Doing Too Little)
Loses sight of goals and objectives.	Establishes clear goals and objectives, taking into account the needs of others.	Fails to establish daily, weekly, and long-term goals.
Is so flexible that goals may not be met on time.	Maintains flexibility but keeps an eye on due dates and priorities.	Doesn't prepare back-up for emergency situations.
Sees the big picture without considering the specifics or practical implications.	Shows equal concern for the big picture and the details.	Doesn't anticipate potential pitfalls or problems.
	Sets priorities and exhibits a sense of urgency.	
	Trains back-up.	

Game Plan for Improving Organization and Planning

- Write a to-do list on a daily basis, and use a tickler file to pull up important dates and deadlines.
- Use others in your work group to set priorities and brainstorm options.
- Block out uninterrupted time for essential tasks.
- Organize your desk and office.
- Keep a notebook with you to take notes and capture important ideas.
- Take a time management class and use time management materials.

You'll notice nowhere does this table say that a person is doing anything wrong. It says the person is out of bounds for your particular playing field, and you want to get him or her back onto the field. There's another way to do this that is equally acceptable and just as effective that doesn't use the sports analogy. Consider what you would like followers to continue doing, what they need to do more of, and what they need to do less of. Put that into a matrix. Here's what the same performance assessment would look like:

MODEL FOR GIVING BEHAVIORAL FEEDBACK

Continue	Do More	Do Less
• Being flexible. • Employing creative, out-of-the-box thinking. • Understanding concepts and the connections between ideas.	• Establishing realistic daily, weekly, and long-term goals. • Preparing backup for emergencies. • Balancing strategic planning and thinking with developing practical execution strategies.	• Getting caught up in analysis paralysis. • Sacrificing goal achievement while striving for perfection.

By removing "right" and "wrong" from the equation, you're less likely to get behavioral extremes in response to your coaching. For example, when one woman was told that she was too aggressive in meetings, she went to the opposite extreme and wouldn't talk at all. In another case, a man who was told he didn't work hard enough suddenly started coming in before everyone else and leaving after everyone else. Even with all the extra hours, though, he still wasn't providing the leader with what she wanted because the leader wasn't specific enough. This is what happens when you (1) label, and (2) give employees only part of the picture. They're left to guess what appropriate behavior might be, often going to an extreme in an effort to change. For people to move incrementally toward effective behavior, the boundaries must be identified first. Then they can be given concrete suggestions for how to approach in-bounds behavior.

I must admit that a world in which no one went out of bounds would be a dull place to live. In fact, nearly everyone goes out of bounds now and then. In a football game when the ball lands out of bounds, time is called and no points are gained for this particular play. The players may huddle to reevaluate what needs to be done next, and the play resumes, hopefully with a new move that yields the desired result—touchdown! The coach doesn't use a foul as an opportunity to punish or discipline a player. He may even applaud him for taking a risk. Instead, he uses it during practice to coach the player toward new behavior. No one's career is threatened over a few lousy plays. Overall, players need more wins than losses to remain on the team, and they can't go out of bounds too frequently, but the coach uses errors, fouls, and mistakes as coaching opportunities.

In business, leaders are often much less forgiving. When employees go out of bounds, they are rarely given the kind of coaching that players get on the field. Employees are lucky if they get yearly performance reviews, let alone regular coaching. The leader as coach often has tremendous difficulty translating a generalized feeling about poor performance into specific coaching tips. Players may go along making mistakes game after game without ever being told what they're doing wrong and what to do to improve the situation.

If you've done everything that's been suggested thus far, the coaching conversation won't be that hard for you. When people trust you and know you have their best interests at heart, they'll be open to what you have to say with the knowledge that you're not punishing them, but rather looking for ways to develop and prepare them for their next assignment. There are essentially three parts of the coaching conversation:

- **What** behaviors are not acceptable.
- **Why** changing the behaviors would benefit the follower.
- **How** new behaviors can be achieved.

Let's take a look at how each of those elements might sound in a broader conversation.

What Behaviors Are Not Acceptable

Leader: I'd like to talk to you about some concerns I have with your relationships with your clients and coworkers. I've noticed some behaviors that I think are impeding your ability to service our clients to the maximum of your potential.

Follower: You've got to be kidding. I'm the best systems guy that you've got.

Leader: Technically, yes. I'm a big admirer of your ability to size up problems and implement solutions. But when it comes to building the kinds of relationships with people that enhance the ability to do the job over the long haul, there are some areas that require your attention.

Follower: I'm not here to win a popularity contest. I want to do the job and do it well. If anyone has any complaints, it's because they can't understand the logic behind the system and are blaming me. I can't help it if they're too dumb to understand.

Leader: To tell you the truth, right now with me you're acting consistent with how I've seen you act with our clients. I'm trying to tell you something and you're not listening to me because you're so busy defending yourself and putting others down. I feel as if I'm not being heard. If I feel that way and we have a *good* relationship, can you imagine how the clients may feel?

Follower: I'm listening.

Why Changing the Behaviors Would Benefit the Follower

Leader: You're a young guy and have a lot of career runway ahead of you. This ability to effectively manage relationships won't help you just today, but for the rest of your career. If you look around our company, you'll notice it's not always the most technically proficient people who get promoted. I'd hate to see you limited in any way by not having the broadest skill set possible.

How Those Behaviors Can Be Achieved

Leader: Let's start now by identifying some specific things you can do beginning today. I'm not saying I'm an expert at all this, so I'd like to hear what you think you might do that would help with the things I've mentioned.

Follower: Well, I guess it wouldn't be that hard to keep my mouth shut more often and listen.

Leader: Listening isn't as easy as it sounds. I even took a course once in active listening. Would you be interested?

Follower: Sure.

Leader: Okay, check with HR and see when the next one is being offered. Another thing that can really help is to ask people if they feel listened to by you. Pick people you trust. The proof will be not in how *you* feel, but in how others do. How do you think you can reduce some of the jargon you use that seems to confuse others?

Follower: That's a little harder. I'm not sure how to correct that.

Leader: Can I offer some suggestions?

Follower: Shoot.

Leader: A tip someone once gave me was to explain things like I would to my ten-year-old. Put things in the simplest terms possible. If it appears they get it quickly, use a little more sophistication. If you combine this approach with the active listening skills, you'll know when people are and aren't tracking.

Follower: It's worth a try.

Leader: That's all I'm asking. Now, about this business of working on relationships. What do you think you could do differently here?

Follower: My wife always complains about this, too. She thinks I get so involved in studying aviation or working on the computer at home that I don't have time for her. I just don't engage in small talk most of the time.

Leader: Just being aware of the need to change is a start. How often do you go to lunch with a coworker?

Follower: I usually work through lunch.

Leader: I appreciate your dedication, but socializing more will help you get to know people. Some of your coworkers could really use your help on projects but are afraid to ask because you always look so busy or don't seem interested. Carve out a few minutes each day to get to know each one of them on more than a business basis. For example, ask Doreen what kind of season her softball team is having. Or let Joe know how good he looks since he's started his diet.

Follower: I didn't even notice he'd lost weight.

Leader: That's what I mean. You're so busy working, you don't really see people. The idea is to build networks of people who help you get the job done over time. I think if you work on the three things we just discussed—use active listening, explain things in simple terms, and spend more time developing relationships—you'll really have made headway. Don't forget that I'm here to help in any way that I can and will let you know how I see you doing. I care enough about you to want to see you succeed. Do I have your commitment to go ahead and give it a shot?

Follower: Okay.

Leader: Great. Why don't we sit down again in about two weeks to see how it's going?

Follower: How about over lunch?

Leader: You're a quick learner.

The leader in this example actually modeled the behavior she expects from the follower. She listened to him, showed concern for him as a person, and broke her message down into simple behavioral components. She even used the behavior in the room as a teaching opportunity—for instance, in her comment "I feel as if I'm not being heard." The leader must now continue to observe the follower as he tries to implement the behaviors outlined. The follower will most likely not go out and be Mr. Personality—that's not who he is. But as the leader sees him approximate the desired changes, she must occasionally reinforce the attempts with verbal, or written, praise. If they're in a meeting together where the follower lapses into using too much jargon or not listening, the leader has the perfect opportunity to sit down with him afterward and provide more coaching examples.

Preparing in advance for the coaching session is often a step that is entirely overlooked, but one that will make a significant impact on how the talk goes. Without preparation, you're more likely to be sidetracked by the follower's comments or by feelings of insecurity when the time comes to deliver the message. There's a certain confidence that comes with preparation. If necessary, role-play the scenario with a friend or spouse. Get feedback on how you can come across more effectively. Above all, let your genuine concern for the follower come through in your delivery. As one woman expressed during a coaching workshop: "Be tough on the problem but gentle on the people."

WHEN COACHING DOESN'T DO THE JOB

I'm often asked, "Does this coaching business really work?" It depends on what is meant by *work*. If the real question is "Does coaching get people to do what I want them to in the way I want them to do it?" then the answer is no. Coaching isn't designed to do that. It's designed to help people draw on their strengths and develop alternative behaviors that allow them to meet their obligations and responsibilities in an acceptable manner—not necessarily as *you* would do it.

On the other hand, there's a consideration that Bill Walsh, former head coach of the San Francisco 49ers, brought up. With any team of players, you'll have one or two superstars who will go far and fast without much coaching from you. Positive rein- forcement and a little redirection now and then are all they need to be at the top of their games. Then you'll have another one or two players who, with targeted coaching in some strategic areas, can get to the superstar level. In the middle of the pack will be three or four players who'll never be superstars, but with ongoing coaching will be solid and dependable players. These are the people who will require most of your coaching energy. And finally, there will always be one or two people on the team who won't respond no matter how much coaching you provide them with.

The only way to know if coaching will work is to coach. You can't predict how someone will respond; you have to do it. Once you've provided coaching (and sometimes technical training) and it hasn't worked, *then* you have to revert to finding ways to do what the British call "freeing people up to find new opportunities." I be- lieve that if you coach and provide training in good faith, then an ultimate decision to terminate a player from the team will likewise be made in good faith. I call this process "decision by looking in the mirror." If you can look yourself in the mirror the morning after a termination, chances are you gave the follower every op- portunity to improve but it was not within his or her realm of capability or desire to change.

Here comes the hard part: that difficult conversation with fol- lowers letting them know their performance is not up to accept- able standards and it's time for them to be looking for their next job. In more than two decades in the field of human resources, I've found that when you're frustrated and at your wit's end with em- ployees, they usually feel the same way but don't know what to do about it. Coaching extends beyond performance development to career guidance. Once again, it's difficult to do if you haven't built trusting relationships.

Coaching someone out of a job can be done with the utmost respect and compassion, but ultimately it's up to the other person to find the solution. When the truth is spoken, there's often a sense of relief on the part of both the leader and the follower. If you've been a conscientious coach, it should also come as no surprise. I believe that people don't fail to meet expectations because they're not smart or capable—they fail because they're not doing what they love, or their own values aren't aligned with those of the leader or the organization. That's why it's important that when you coach the person out of a job, the conversation be focused not on faultfinding but rather on helping the person to find a more suitable situation that would use his or her unique talents and interests. Here's how such a conversation might go:

Leader: Chris, I want to talk to you about your performance. For the past year, you and I have worked together to achieve some specific goals. I'm frustrated because you're just not doing the things we agreed upon and I don't know what more I can do to help you. How do you see the situation?

Follower: I've tried—I really have. But it just doesn't come naturally to me to do the things we've discussed. I feel as if I'm being asked to be someone I'm not.

Leader: I can understand how you might feel that way. You certainly have many strengths that I value, but they're not enough to ensure long-term success. To be successful in this organization, you really have to be more versatile. I think that will be true in most situations, but if you don't want to change, then you're going to have to find a position that allows you to stay in your comfort zone.

Follower: Are you firing me?

Leader: I'm saying you're not meeting the goals we established together, to which you committed, and that we've worked on for more than a year. Now it's time for us to discuss how you're going to transition to your next job. I know you're just as frustrated as I am, and what I want is to help you find a position that will allow you to be more of who you are.

Follower: So what does that mean?

Leader: It means I want us to come up with a reasonable separation date for you and to talk about how I can help you in finding new employment.

Follower: I didn't realize it was so serious.

Leader: I'm not sure how you could have missed the clues. I've been direct and straightforward every step of the way. We even have coaching plans and two past performance reviews that show your performance isn't up to standard. What I'd like you to do is take the rest of the day off—you'll be paid for it—and come in tomorrow prepared to discuss what you'd like to do. If you have a résumé, bring it in and I'll have a friend who does career counseling clean it up and make suggestions for how you can put together a job search. I'll also give you time off with pay to interview. I really want to help you find something you'll be happier with. I know the job market is tight, so I'm willing to keep you on the payroll for two months or until you find a job—whichever comes first. If you prefer, I can arrange to give you two months' severance and Friday can be your last day—but I'll leave that choice up to you. If you choose to stay, though, you're going to have to meet certain goals and maintain your professionalism.

You get the idea. Allowing people to save face and finding win-win solutions to this tough situation is critical not only for the employee but also for you and the organization as well. If you treat followers fairly and with dignity and respect, you'll reduce the likelihood of unwanted ramifications or legal challenges related to the separation.

Coaching, then, is about empowering others to succeed—not only with what they're currently doing but also with what they're not doing but might like to. Leaders who intuitively know that followers who are not satisfied with whatever it is they're doing—whether it's serving on a committee, working for a company, or volunteering with a nonprofit agency—should coach the follower in a direction that ultimately helps the leader, follower, and organization to move forward. Coaches who have built a solid and trusting relationship with followers can do this with little difficulty.

Let me end this chapter with an inventory you can take to assess your current level of coaching capability. If you're really brave, you can give it to your followers to complete and return to you anonymously so that you get their viewpoint as well. With a little tweaking, you can even use it with your children or others for whom you have coaching or leadership responsibility.

COACHING EFFECTIVENESS INVENTORY

Scale:

1 = Almost Always

3 = Sometimes

2 = Usually

4 = Rarely

To what extent do you:

1. _____ Let people know on a regular, informal basis how they are doing?

2. _____ Provide people with immediate feedback for their performance (both positive and negative)?

3. _____ Take the time to observe specific behaviors of your followers that contribute to or detract from their effectiveness?

4. _____ Tell people exactly what behaviors require change and what the desired behavior looks like?

5. _____ Know the goals and interests of your followers?

6. _____ Take time for casual conversation with your followers?

7. _____ Know enough about the personal lives of your followers to understand the impact on their work performance?

8. _____ Feel comfortable personally confronting followers about behaviors you think are inappropriate or counterproductive?

9. _____ Know what each of your followers is most proud of?

10. _____ Build individual relationships with your followers?

11. _____ Illuminate follower strengths and weaknesses so that they can see them for themselves?

12. _____ Listen to individuals about their feelings, ideas, or concerns?

13. _____ Assist followers with ways of building on their strengths and improving areas of weakness?

14. _____ Feel comfortable acting as an impartial listener to a follower with a personal problem?

15. _____ Think that followers believe that you act in their best interest?

16. _____ Adapt your coaching style to meet the specific skill levels and needs of individuals?

17. _____ Build strong teams with complementary strengths?

18. _____ Set realistic targets and goals for individuals as well as for the team?

19. _____ Encourage followers to take personal and team responsibility for stewardship for getting the entire job done?

20. _____ Delegate the desired outcome without trying to control the process?

Now add up the numbers. How did you do? The lower your score, the better, on this instrument. Use the following scale to give you an idea of how effectively you're currently using coaching.

If Your Score Is . . .

20–30 You exhibit high coaching behavior. You do a good job of letting people know where they stand, encouraging employees to excel, and building the kinds of relationships that enable you to successfully lead your team. You understand the points I'm making and may even have been able to write a few chapters yourself. Keep up the good work!

31–55 You exhibit moderate coaching behavior. At times you provide employees with the kind of guidance they want and need, but you are hesitant to confront and delve deeply into the tougher issues and concerns of your people. Let your hair down more often, get to know your staff, and let them get to know you. Don't be afraid of getting too close—employees will let you know if you do. It's better to err on the side of caring too much than too little.

56–80 You exhibit low coaching behavior. You've got your nose to the grindstone too much. Stop *doing* so much and start *being* more. Leadership involves really knowing the people who report to you on more than a superficial level. Part of your job as a leader is to develop your people. Until you do this, you'll only be able to manage, not lead.

Coaching Tips for the Leader As Coach

39. *Build a trusting relationship with each member of your team.* Trust forms the foundation for coaching. Without it, attempts to give feedback will be viewed as critical or just wanting to get more work out of a person. Showing a genuine concern for people, listening openly to their concerns, and knowing what matters to them will put you on the road to creating trust.

40. *Practice the 7:1 Rule—seven pieces of positive feedback for every piece of developmental feedback.* When followers do a good job on a project, let them know specifically what you liked or appreciated. Don't overlook the small

things—you want people to do those things well, too. Keep in mind the three caveats of positive reinforcement: It has to be genuine, specific, and free from implied criticism.

41. **Clearly define and communicate your expectations.** People aren't mind readers; nor do they *want* to fail. Begin with the assumption *If they knew better, they'd do better,* and provide direction about what you need from them.

42. **Assess less-than-acceptable performance or behaviors in neutral terms.** Avoid characterizations such as *lazy, not a team player, disorganized,* or *aloof.* Instead, pretend you have a video camera trained on people and describe what it can actually see them doing. Use the in-bounds and out-of-bounds model to define what they're doing too much of or too little of and what the camera would see if they were working in a more acceptable way.

43. **Stretch your followers.** One of the messages I have heard consistently over the years is that followers appreciate leaders who stretch them to go beyond their self-imposed limitations. This is contrary to the way in which many leaders mistakenly allow staff to perform indefinitely at their comfort level. If they're meeting your expectations, you may figure, *Why tamper with a good thing?* The reason why is that a good coach knows her players need to be challenged if they are to remain competitive, motivated, and vital to the organization and the team. One of the best stretching exercises you can give a follower is to delegate one of your own responsibilities. Just remember, though—*what you were responsible for before you delegated it, you're responsible for after you delegated it.* When giving a stretch assignment, be sure to observe behavior, provide feedback, and redirect as needed.

44. **Differentiate coaching from discipline.** Coaching, done properly, eliminates the need for discipline except in the most egregious circumstances. The model taught to many leaders for progressive discipline is designed to protect organizations from unwarranted liability, not to create peak performers. Use it as a last resort. Coaching, done constantly and consistently, will take good players and make them even better.

45. **Prepare your coaching conversations.** A little forethought helps to make a coaching session more effective. Each coaching conversation should include a description of what, why, and how: *what* behaviors are less than acceptable; *why* it would benefit the person to make the changes; and *how* the person can successfully achieve the goals.

46. **Use interim performance reviews as an entrée to coaching.** One of the biggest mistakes leaders make is to provide a follower with a performance review that contains developmental feedback he or she has never heard before. You can prevent this by simply taking the organization's standard performance review form, completing it, and using it for talking points during a coaching session. Assure the follower that this is not something that will go into the personnel file, but that you do want to be clear about strengths and areas for development.

47. **Coach players who are mismatched for the job out of the organization or current position.** People don't fail because they're stupid or lazy; they fail because they're not a good match for a job or the situation. They often possess valuable talents that aren't being well utilized, or that the current job doesn't require. Keeping these people on board can create morale problems for the rest of the team. Use coaching to

help them to identify what they would rather be doing and exit their positions with dignity.

48. ***Hone your coaching skills.*** Like anything else, coaching can be learned and must be practiced to gain confidence and competence in it. Start by honestly assessing your coaching skills and getting input from others about what they need from you. Then learn as much as you can about coaching by attending workshops, reading books, and practicing the skills provided in this chapter.

49. ***Read* The Set-Up-to-Fail Syndrome** by Jean-François Manzoni and Jean-Louis Barsoux. The subtitle, *How Good Managers Cause Great People to Fail,* really says it all. Whether you lead a team of corporate employees or a group of volunteers, the authors provide tangible examples of the ways in which you might be sabotaging the best efforts of your followers.

CHAPTER SIX

Leading Teams:
From the PTA to the Boardroom

Teamwork is what makes common people capable of achieving uncommon results.

—Pat Summitt, head coach of the
University of Tennessee Lady Vols

You've already led a team if you've:

- Raised or are raising a family.
- Led a committee or task force.
- Organized a potluck dinner.
- Created a book club.
- Directed a community play.
- Mobilized people to take political action.

Women understand the concept of teamwork at its most fundamental level. Even if you've never played a sport or managed a
department, I'm certain there have been times when you've coor-
dinated the efforts of groups of people to achieve a common goal.
Whereas men cognitively know that teamwork is essential to long-
term success, you're more likely to possess the skills needed to make
it a reality. Women's sense of fair play, desire to create communities
of interest, ability to draw out the individual talents of others, and

willingness to admit their own shortcomings all contribute to the outstanding ability to be strong team leaders.

Women's team-building skills are most often seen in the community, philanthropic, and nonprofit organizations they've historically been responsible for starting and running. The Parent Teacher Association (PTA), Mothers Against Drunk Driving (MADD), the American Red Cross, and Planned Parenthood were all founded and remain largely run by women. They began with a vision, then harnessed the talents of others to become institutions.

There may be no better place to examine the role of women as team builders than by looking at Assistance League. Founded in 1894 by Anne Banning, Assistance League today is a vibrant nonprofit organization with a mission to "put caring and commitment into action through community-based philanthropic projects." It is run almost entirely by volunteers, with 117 chapters and more than 24,000 members nationwide. Operation School Bell is its national signature program, providing new clothing as well as health and hygiene kits to 135,000 disadvantaged schoolchildren annually. I became familiar with the group when I gave a keynote presentation on leadership at its annual conference. The energy, enthusiasm, and organizational skills of the women I met gave me renewed respect for what a team of committed and well-led volunteers can achieve. Judy Mullin, the league's national president, took the time to share with me her secrets for leading a team of volunteers—which, in the end, are the same things you must do no matter what kind of group you lead. I started off by asking her how she became a leader:

> *I never thought about being a leader. I was involved in student*
> *government in college and was president of a number of volun-*

teer organizations, but I always saw myself as a contributor to the process, not a leader. Each opportunity to lead sounded like a new adventure and I got swept up in the process—which is the reward itself.

Over the years I learned that to lead a team, you have to start with a common goal. You have to make sure everyone is going in the same direction—but people have different talents. It's my job as a leader to take those talents and abilities and fit them into the bigger puzzle. You can't do this well unless you have clearly defined your expectations and set norms—made sure everyone knows what is expected of them and who's doing what. My job is made easier by the fact that the organization has a strong infrastructure, good training programs, and opportunities for networking. All of these factors combine to create commitment from the team members because they know there's a network of support behind them if they need help. That's key. Once people know they have support, they know they can reach the goal. I've done things I never dreamed of doing because I knew I had support.

My local chapter once needed a treasurer, and no one stepped up to fill the spot. I said if not one living soul will do it, I will. I was completely out of my element and it was the most challenging leadership experience of my life, but together we revamped a financial system that really needed it. Even though I was the leader of the project, I couldn't have done it alone. I was learning every step of the way. If a leader doesn't continually learn, she's not a very effective leader.

I'm also a big believer in communicating on a regular basis because it makes people feel connected. To be successful, leaders have to create a connection among the members and encourage communication. I talk to the other team members a lot about it *and create consciousness that team members need to stay aware of what the others are doing.*

If I were to give young leaders some suggestions, they would be to read as much about leadership as you can, be open, ask questions, and don't hesitate to try something. If you think something needs to be done, you've got to try. When something isn't working, try to figure out how to make it work. It's incredibly rewarding.

Judy's leadership path is similar to that of many other women. She started off by leading small groups or projects; as she was presented with new opportunities to lead, she realized that these were learning experiences to embrace, not avoid. As the leader of one of this nation's largest, most respected, and best-run organizations, she focuses on what's important: *a clear goal, expressly stated expectations, tapping into the talents of individual members, and constant communication.*

INSTILLING TEAMWORK

With more than 880 career wins, Pat Summitt, head coach of the University of Tennessee Lady Vols, is literally the "winningest" college basketball coach—male or female—in history. Coach Summitt knows how to develop winners. Twelve of her players went on to become Olympians, and twenty have played professional basketball after playing for her. Regardless of whether you're leading a project, a department, or an entire organization, you can learn something from Coach Summitt. She writes about the secret of her success in her book *Reach for the Summit:*

> *Teamwork is taught. You don't just lump a group of people together in a room and call them a team and expect them to behave*

like one. No organization will succeed without teamwork, no matter how many all-stars you have. I talk about teamwork until I have no voice left. Without an incentive people simply won't work together consistently. But if you can grasp the real incentive behind teamwork, instilling it suddenly becomes a lot easier: Teamwork is not a matter of persuading yourself and your colleagues to set aside personal ambition for the greater good. It's a matter of recognizing that your personal ambitions and the ambitions of the team are one and the same. *That's the incentive.*

Reading this gives you an idea of how Coach Summitt has racked up so many wins in her coaching career. When I coach new leaders, I tell them that one of the very first things they must do is clearly communicate their expectations for teamwork. I personally do it not only on my own team at Corporate Coaching International, but even when I serve on a committee—whether I'm leading it or not. You begin by creating a set of *mutually developed and agreed-upon* guidelines for team behavior. You say to the team, "One of the things that's really important to me is that we work collaboratively as a team. To do this we need to come up with some 'rules of the road' for how we're going to interact." At first you may get some blank stares, so be prepared to explain that the purpose of the guidelines is to make it safe for everyone on the team to participate fully and contribute to their full potential so that the team benefits from the power of collaboration. You may have to kick it off with some of your own ideas for how the team should behave. Make sure you don't make this *your* list by providing each and every guideline. It's got to be the *team's* list.

Some of the items that typically appear on lists of the rules of the road include:

- Meetings will begin and end on time.
- Everyone is expected to fully participate.
- There are no bad ideas—anything that's put on the table gets discussed.
- Be conscious of how much airtime you take up.
- Invite quieter members to speak up.
- Cell phones, BlackBerrys, and pagers are turned off.
- Play by Las Vegas rules: *What's said and done here, stays here* (unless permission is otherwise granted).
- Each team member is responsible for helping colleagues achieve their goals.
- There are to be no complaints—concerns must be accompanied by a solution or request for help with finding one.
- Everyone is expected to attend team meetings with the exception of urgent business-related activities.

Once the team has developed the list, have it printed on notepads, made into posters for the meeting room, or in other ways made a visible and integral part of team meetings. It lets the team members know you're serious about abiding by these rules. Similarly, now you have a tool you can use to measure team performance. And when it comes to either individual or team behavior, *what you measure is what you get.* In the event that you're the formal team leader, you should also tell members that their individual performance will be measured, in part, by the degree to which they contribute to the success of the team. If particular team members decide meetings aren't important and don't attend, it's fair game to first give them feedback that they're not meeting your expectations; if they still don't take you seriously, have the issue appear on a performance review as an area for development. As a leader, you must hold people accountable for living by the guidelines. If you don't, people will think you really don't care—and I guarantee you'll see teamwork erode and eventually collapse.

When you're leading a project team, it's pretty easy to identify ways in which the team can work interdependently. When you're leading a department with a variety of functions, it can be a little tougher—but not impossible. Let me give you an example. Roberta is the board chair for a nonprofit organization. The board has committees that correspond with the organization's various functions, including finance, donor development, corporate relations, and community relations. Each committee is responsible for overseeing those functions. If Roberta wasn't concerned with teamwork, she could allow each of the committees to function independently and just report back to the full board with little input from the others. But she is concerned, because she understands that high-performing boards use synergy to maximize the collective wisdom and skills of the team. The basic concept of synergy is that the collective energy, wisdom, or output of a team exceeds the simple sum of the team's parts. It's a case of $1 + 1 + 1 + 1 + 1 \neq 5$ but exponentially more than that.

To achieve this synergy, Roberta works with the board to identify interdependent goals such as reviewing marketing materials together, with the community relations and corporate relations committees collaborating on printed material. Similarly, finance committee members need to know when a donor drive is conducted so that they can oversee the systems for receiving contributions. Each committee needs to be involved with media campaigns to ensure that communications coming out of the board and the organization are seamless and without any kind of overlap that would make it appear that the left hand doesn't know what the right hand is doing.

A big part of creating team synergy comes from clearly defined roles and responsibilities and constant communication among groups within the department. Roberta makes good use of board meetings to ensure a consistent flow of information throughout the entire board. Many leaders fail to understand the purpose of team meetings and how to maximize them in building a high-functioning, cohesive team.

MEETING MANAGEMENT

One of the reasons why people hate team meetings so much is that many team leaders don't have a clue how to run an efficient and productive meeting. There's nothing more frustrating than to have a pile of work on your desk, yet be required to sit for endless hours in an unproductive meeting. Or to leave your home on a cold night and drive across town in traffic, only to attend a meeting of volunteers where nothing ever gets accomplished. That's when you see the BlackBerrys turn on and team members check out. Keep in mind that team meetings are designed to:

- Allow the team leader to share information of general interest to team members.
- Encourage team members to share with one another information of general interest.
- Provide time for updates on the status of major projects.
- Give the team the opportunity to address and resolve issues of concern to all members.
- Provide an environment to build interdependent relationships that help the team to reach its collective goals.

With this in mind, here are some dos and don'ts to help you effectively lead team meetings:

EFFECTIVE TEAM MEETINGS

Do	Don't
Develop an agenda in advance by soliciting discussion topics in advance of each meeting.	Come to meetings unprepared.
Have ground rules that create safety for members.	Allow one or two people to dominate discussions.
Allot time frames to each agenda topic.	Allow conversations to continue that should take place offline.
Allow time on the agenda to address each item listed above.	Go over your scheduled end time.
Have a flip chart or white board available at each meeting.	Rely on your memory to capture important information, takeaways, or to-dos.
Rotate the roles of scribe, timekeeper, and facilitator.	Feel as if *you* have to be in charge of meetings, rather than sharing ownership and responsibility for the success of team meetings.
Meet no less than biweekly — and make meeting times sacrosanct (departmental teams).	Cancel meetings at the last minute or because not everyone can attend.
Use the project status sheet to update progress on key projects.	Use valuable meeting time for people to report on everything they're doing day to day.
Begin and end the meeting on time.	Wait for everyone to show up before starting.
Re-calendar issues that could not be completed within the time frame allotted, and schedule new issues for subsequent meetings.	Remain on topics that are better discussed one-to-one.

What would an agenda look like? Here's a sample that you can tailor to meet the unique needs of your team. Within each major topic, use bullets to enter items you want to cover and those that team members have submitted for discussion—each with times attached. For example, if people want to discuss a particular problem, they should indicate how much time on the agenda they need. Attaching time frames and sticking with them are crucial for ensuring that the meeting runs efficiently and ends on time.

TEAM AGENDA FOR JUNE 22 MEETING

9:00 AM   Report from Team Leader

This is where you provide information on things happening within the organization that impact team members. Typically, this information comes from meetings you attend or sources the other team members may not have access to. Examples of items in your report might be related to new hires, shifts in the organization's direction, new clients or customers, new systems that will be implemented by the organization, or mandates from senior management.

9:15 AM   What's the Buzz

Individual team members often have information of which the team leader and their colleagues may not be aware. It can be as simple as noting that today is someone's birthday or a rumor they want to dispel. This fifteen-minute portion of the agenda is simply time for the team to share general information that impacts them.

9:30 AM   Project Status Report

Using the Project Status Sheet below, progress toward and obstacles to *mutual* goals are reported. This is not a time to go around the room and have everyone discuss what they're working on. This is a mistake that many leaders make; it causes members to tune out. A detailed discussion of individual progress toward goals is something you do one-on-one with each of your followers offline. You should encourage people to pass if there's nothing to report.

10:00 AM   **Collaborative Problem Solving and Information Sharing**
This portion of the agenda is used to discuss sticky situations team members may be facing and need help with, concerns they have about team issues, or things they have learned (books, articles, workshops they've attended) that could benefit the other team members.

10:30 AM   **Adjourn**

If you haven't been in the habit of holding team meetings, or team meetings in this format, people will need time to get used to it. At first they may not submit agenda items, but if they find there's no time on the agenda to discuss what they want, they'll soon learn how to do it. If it appears there's not enough time to discuss a particular item, it should be rescheduled for further discussion at the next meeting; alternatively, if it appears the subject is more pertinent to some people than others, those involved should agree to meet offline.

The following Project Status Sheet can be used as a template for capturing major team activities that require discussion at meetings. You can tailor it to more closely suit your needs, but it forms the foundation for keeping abreast of progress and identifying areas that need more attention from you. Items remain on the sheet until they've been completed and new ones added as you go along and the sheet is updated after each meeting.

PROJECT STATUS SHEET

Project	Point Person(s)	Anticipated Date of Completion	Current Status	Other
Design marketing materials	Craig & Erica	8/30	Designer has submitted first draft Printers are submitting quotes	
Develop financial accounting systems	Peter & Chris	9/15	Department managers meeting scheduled for week of 7/7	Awaiting approved format from VP of Finance
Department off-site	LaShawn, David, & Kim	10/12	Contract signed with hotel Facilitator is designing program for team review Team survey will be distributed next week	

TRUSTLESS TEAMS

Team leaders often call me to help repair teams where trust is an issue. The leader is often baffled by how such lack of trust came to pass. The fact is, trustless teams don't just happen, they're created—often by leaders. They do it by not communicating their expectations about teamwork, encouraging competition among members, not taking the time to meet with team members individually or collectively, and allowing team problems to fester. You usually know when a team isn't working synergistically, but here is a list of trustless team symptoms that may help confirm your suspicions:

- **Cliques:** Subgroups of team members that exclude others.

- **Poor communication habits:** Lack of openness, reluctance to explore team members' concerns, unwillingness to truly listen.

- **Inflexibility:** Team members dogmatically sticking to their perceptions and beliefs, even in the face of contrary evidence.

- **Lack of respect:** Concerns about team members' competence, knowledge, or motives.

- **Guarded information flow:** Excessive control of information and information processes.

- **Hidden agendas:** Objectives and expectations that are not freely shared.

- **Avoidance of conflict:** Lack of interpersonal confrontation about legitimate concerns.

- **Backbiting:** Critical discussions of team members behind their backs.

- **Backstabbing or sabotage:** Attempts to undermine the credibility or success of a team member.

- **End-arounds:** Avoiding or eliminating someone who should legitimately be involved in a decision, request, or communication.

- **Inappropriate independence:** Stubbornly refusing to seek the input of other team members or to work toward consensus.

- **Poor follow-through:** Failure to keep commitments or take agreed-on actions.

- **Disinterest:** Displaying apathy, indifference, or inattention to team activities.

- **Contradictory goals:** Team members heading in individually determined and different directions.

- **Responsibility gaps or overlaps:** Misaligned roles or behaviors.

If a team that you're responsible for leading is experiencing these symptoms, then it's imperative that you do something about it. *How* you do it is the tricky part. The simple fact that there *is* a lack of trust creates a situation where team members are skeptical about any efforts to turn the situation around. Members may feel as if they have already tried to make it better and no one cares. The tension among team members makes it hard to get them to feel safe enough to talk about it. No matter how well-intentioned (or skilled in team building) the team leader is, my recommendation is to get outside help. The team leader is also a member of the team and, as such, is part of the problem—often more so than she may even realize. A *seasoned* outside facilitator will create an environment where team members' concerns can be aired freely and thoroughly.

If you work in a large organization, you may have a human resource or training department that can be of help. If so, ask for their assistance with designing and facilitating an off-site team-building program. If not, talk to some other leaders in your community to get references for outside consultants who can help you with moving your team forward. Depending on how severe the problem is within your team, you will want to be certain the facilitator is capable of handling difficult situations—someone who can focus not only on the superficial aspects of the problem but also on the deeper issues that contributed to the problem initially and that now preclude the team from working together effectively. Having facilitated hundreds of team-building programs during my career, I know the process can be painful for everyone involved. The last thing you need is someone who doesn't have the experience to help teams that are bogged down in the quagmire of fear, anger, tension, and frustration.

You can prevent getting to the point of no return by doing much of what I've already discussed in this chapter. Something else you can do is conduct a team assessment to take the temperature of your team and use it as the basis for a team building. The team survey that follows is relatively easy to administer, yet yields valuable results. There are a few caveats associated with conducting any kind of climate survey:

- **Anonymity must be assured if you want honest responses:** Allow people to complete the survey and return it in the manner that provides them with the most comfort. Some people will be willing to return it by e-mail, but others may want the anonymity that fax or mail allows.

- **Share results with the team:** If you sanitize the data, people won't trust you or your intentions. Part of creating a high-performing team is being willing to expose the good, the bad, and the ugly in an effort to make things better. That's why you want people to know in advance that the data will be shared so that they can avoid examples or jargon that would point to them. They may ultimately be willing to identify themselves as responsible for a particular piece of feedback, but that choice should be theirs.

- **Be prepared to take action:** There's nothing worse than being asked for your opinion, providing an honest response, then having it ignored. That will lead to even more problems, as team members will think you don't care enough to make a good situation better or correct a bad situation.

- **Make team building a priority:** I often chuckle to myself when I get a call from a client with a team in crisis who wants a team-building program conducted in one day in the office conference room. What kind of message does that give to the team members about how important this is? If you're going to do it, do it right. Creating a safe environment free from distractions, getting all the issues on the table, teaching team skills, and developing a "back-home" action plan take time. That's why I only facilitate programs that are at least two days long and held at an off-site location—preferably one far enough away from the office that a sleepover is required.

- **Don't expect immediate results:** Your team didn't get to where it is—good *or* bad—overnight. Neither does bringing the team to the next level of play. That's why you want to make any takeaways from your team-building program an integral part of your team's day-to-day planning and follow-up.

- **Hold people accountable:** Team-building programs aren't designed to create fond memories—although it's nice when they do. They're designed to *create significant and enduring change* within the team. All too often, companies spend thousands of dollars on feel-good retreats, the results of which last about two days once everyone gets back to the ranch. That's why it's your job as the leader to hold people accountable for implementing the systems or practicing the skills covered during the off-site. Remember: *What you measure is what you get.*

TEAM EFFECTIVENESS SURVEY

Part I

Instructions: For the purpose of this survey, your team consists of everyone who works within the XYZ Department reporting to Jane Doe. Using the scale 1 = *not descriptive of our team,* through 10 = *highly descriptive of our team,* answer each of the following questions as candidly as possible. You should not put your name on the form—all responses are anonymous.

1.   Communication

Team members freely consult with one another, and there are thorough and in-depth discussions about issues impacting the team.

1   2   3   4   5   6   7   8   9   10

2.   Decision Making

Solutions to problems and decisions are arrived at by facts and opinions being thoroughly discussed as opposed to one or two people making decisions for the entire team.

1   2   3   4   5   6   7   8   9   10

3.   Confronting

Problems are confronted on a regular basis and explored in depth with respect shown for differing opinions or ideas.

1   2   3   4   5   6   7   8   9   10

4.   Initiative

Everyone exhibits responsibility for introducing new ideas for solving team problems.

1   2   3   4   5   6   7   8   9   10

5.   Standards of Excellence

Standards used to judge team effectiveness and accomplishments are clearly defined and receive commitment from all team members.

1   2   3   4   5   6   7   8   9   10

6.   Belonging

Group members take the time to understand one another and make everyone feel like an integral part of the team

1   2   3   4   5   6   7   8   9   10

7.   Trust

Team members trust one another and feel safe enough to openly discuss most matters

    1   2   3   4   5   6   7   8   9   10

8.   Pride

Team members exhibit pride not just in their own work but also in that of others.

    1   2   3   4   5   6   7   8   9   10

9.   Critique

Team members take time to give each other feedback (both positive and developmental) about how they are working together.

    1   2   3   4   5   6   7   8   9   10

10.   Interdependence

Team members recognize the need for interdependent working and see that their success is related to the success of others on the team—if one succeeds, we all succeed; if one fails, we all fail.

    1   2   3   4   5   6   7   8   9   10

Part II

Instructions: In this section you are asked to answer four questions. Again, please do so honestly, but understand that your responses will be reported *verbatim*. Therefore, if anonymity is important to you, avoid jargon or phrases that would identify you.

1. What do you like best about this team?
2. What could this team do more of to be even more effective?

3. What could this team do less of to be even more effective?
4. Other comments about your team.

ENCOURAGING AND REWARDING TEAMWORK

Jan Cloyde, an executive vice president at City National Bank, has had a lot of experience with teams—both volunteer and corporate. When I first met her about ten years ago, she was the board president for Big Sisters of Los Angeles; subsequently, she's come to sit on boards of nonprofits such as People Assisting the Homeless and the Executive Women's Group at the Iris Cantor–UCLA Women's Health Center. When I interviewed her for this book, I first asked her what it takes to lead a team of volunteers; I went on to inquire what it takes to lead a team of employees.

Leading a high-performing team really starts with being passionate and positive—that's catching. It's hard for people not to get behind you if you have passion for what you're doing. My passion is about making everybody as successful as they can be— making them want to do what's asked of them. Then it requires setting clear goals, letting people know how you expect them to operate, and treating people with respect. You have to create expectations and lay out the rules and the game plan. You also have to walk the talk. You show by example how you expect people to act on the team. When they do, provide frequent praise. Catch people doing things right and let them know you notice it. When they don't, coach them along the way without making a big deal out of it.

When it comes to leading volunteer teams, you have to assess that the people you have on the team both are committed and have the time to do what's expected of them. They may have the commitment but not the time. Letting people know what's expected and then asking them if they can commit to it is important. So often we assume because someone says they'll do something, they're as committed as we are, when they're not. One of the hardest lessons I've learned as a leader is expecting without inspecting. The more senior you become, the more you expect people to operate in certain ways, but they may or may not do it in the way you need it to be done. That's why in the beginning, you need to observe and review work to make sure it meets your specific expectations.

Jan makes it clear that if you want individuals to behave like a team, they have to be reinforced for doing so *and* held accountable for not doing so. A common practice that I see more among male leaders than female is to create competition among team members so that each will perform better than the next. In the organizations they lead, you often see force-ranked performance reviews: There must be a finite number of people ranked high, a finite number in the middle, and a finite number low. As a woman, I lean toward internal collaboration rather than competition, so I'm not a fan of this rating system. Whether you lead an all-volunteer team, a committee, or a department of a major corporation, team members have to view the *real* competition as being outside the group, not their colleagues.

If you reward people only for their individual achievements, then they will assume teamwork isn't something you value. Many performance review formats measure goal attainment, but not how the goal was reached. This shortsighted approach is what causes many staff members to get the job done at all costs, leaving bodies in their wake. Again—*what you measure is what you get.*

This is why in addition to the rules of the road for team behavior, you should have a written set of *your* expectations related to teamwork, communicate these to the team, and measure people based on their commitment to them. Some specific behaviors you might consider including on your list are:

- Listens to others and tries to understand their feelings before taking action.
- Plans communications effectively so that ideas are clearly understood by others.
- Is sensitive to the morale and feelings of subordinates, colleagues, and management.
- Solicits input from colleagues.
- Exhibits concern for achieving goals with a spirit of cooperation rather than competitiveness.
- Seeks and accepts feedback for improvement without defensiveness.
- Pitches in to assist others whether requested or not.
- Is aware of and adept at organizational politics.
- Is at ease with and courteous to people at all levels.
- Offers constructive criticism rather than being overly critical or minimizing the need for correction.
- Cooperates with others.

Some leaders find rewarding individual performance a lot easier than rewarding team performance. With individuals you can give pats on the back, good performance reviews, gift certificates, raises, bonuses, promotions, and more. But how do you encourage and recognize teamwork? Holding regular team meetings (and calling them *team* meetings, not *staff* meetings) and arranging off-site retreats is a good start, but not enough. In his book *1001 Ways to Reward Employees,* Bob Nelson devotes an entire section to group and team awards. He interviewed hundreds of leaders to learn their best practices when it comes to encouraging teamwork and recognizing employees. Here are just a few of the great suggestions contained in his book:

- When the team accomplishes a particular goal, close down the office for the afternoon and take everyone to a movie and dinner.

- If the team has worked madly to meet a deadline, give everyone gift certificates to a spa so that they can unwind.

- To encourage teamwork across departments, create interdepartmental task forces charged with the task of solving a problem, developing a new product, or designing new systems that leverage the power of teams.

- Responding quickly to and immediately implementing team ideas is also reinforcing and doesn't cost you anything.

- Give team members a disposable camera and have them capture the spirit of teamwork over the course of a week. Then create a slide show with the pictures taken to show to the entire staff.

- Rather than recognize an Employee of the Month, institute a Team of the Month program. Reward the winners with a team dinner, tickets to a sporting event, or gift certificates.

- Have the team work together to develop a team slogan and logo. Then put it on coffee mugs, T-shirts, or tote bags to serve as a reminder that each individual is part of a greater whole.

Coaching Tips for Creating High-Performing Teams

50. **Talk about teamwork—constantly.** Just because you want your team to play nicely together in the sandbox doesn't mean they will. Talk about team goals and your expectations about teamwork at every opportunity.

51. **Define team rules.** Every game has a set of rules by which it operates. Even families have implicit and explicit rules for expected behaviors. Team rules create a safe environment for team members to speak up, be honest, and contribute to their maximum capability. They should be developed *with* the team, not *for* it.

52. **Prepare for team meetings.** Leaders who just show up and wing it will find that team members eventually stop coming because they think the meetings are a waste of their time. Exhibit respect for others' time by making good use of it. Preparing for a meeting includes developing an agenda, outlining what you want to share, and soliciting agenda items from the team.

53. **Manage meetings effectively.** Preparing for meetings isn't enough. You have to be certain that meetings start and end on time, one or two members aren't allowed to dominate the meeting, and limitations are placed on the amount of time you will spend on any one agenda item.

54. **Conduct regular team climate surveys.** Don't repeat the mistake made by many leaders of waiting until there's a crisis before conducting a team survey. That's a little like waiting to go to a marriage counselor until you and your partner can no

longer even speak to each other. An assessment of how team members view the overall functioning of their team, including its leadership, should be done at least once every eighteen months—even if you don't detect any problems. The caveat is that if you're going to do it, you have to take action on the results.

55. **Define measures for team performance.** If you had a videocamera trained on your team, what would you want it to see and hear with regard to team behavior? Write these behaviors down and let people know that getting the job done isn't enough—their performance will also be judged on how well they achieve these less tangible goals.

56. **Identify incentives and rewards for team success.** Read Bob Nelson's books *1001 Ways to Reward Employees* and *1001 Ways to Energize Employees.* They are filled with the best practices of hundreds of organizations large and small.

57. **Create opportunities for team members to work collaboratively.** Committees and project teams comprising cross-functional people provide tangible ways for team members to exchange ideas, hear new viewpoints, and learn about different parts of the organization. It's a great example of the maxim *The message is in the method.*

58. **Hold brainstorming, town hall, or all-hands meetings to encourage cross-functional dialogue.** If you lead a particularly large organization—a department, a board, or the like—this can be an effective way of learning more about what's going on in the organization and communicating messages that everyone hears from you, not through the grapevine. General Electric once offered a program called "the GE Workout." These were regularly scheduled meetings in which

groups of employees from different units were called together to solve a particular organizational problem. Present were senior executives who could immediately give approval to ideas that emerged. It resulted in employees feeling empowered and as if they had ownership of outcomes.

59. **Be an MBWA leader.** That stands for "Managing by Walking Around," and you don't have to be a manager to do it. Let's say you lead a task force within your organization. Taking time to go to the offices of team members (or calling them on the phone if they're not in your building) to discuss their ideas can yield valuable information they might not be willing to share in the full group. Don't "be a girl" and worry that people will view you as having nothing better to do. This is one of the ways that you build a constituency.

60. **Hone your group process skills.** Teams operate on many levels, some transparent (such as focusing on goal attainment) but others more opaque (such as unspoken indicators of morale issues). Your ability as a leader to read both levels accurately is critical to ensuring team success. Consider attending one of NTL's (http://ntl.org) programs related to understanding group process.

CHAPTER SEVEN

A Woman's Secret Weapons: Likability and Emotional Quotients

> Our humanity rests upon a series of learned behaviors, woven together into patterns that are infinitely fragile and never directly inherited.
>
> —Margaret Mead

You've already exhibited likability and a high emotional quotient if you've:

- Built enduring friendships.
- Solicited and taken action on developmental feedback.
- Resolved a conflict with a friend or partner.
- Held your emotions in check in a volatile situation.
- Become sought after as a friend, confidante, or sounding board.
- Attended social events to build your network.

You may have learned in childhood to mind your P's and Q's, but your LQ and EQ are what you should be keeping an eye on if you want to be an effective leader. You probably know that *IQ* refers to "intelligence quotient." Fewer people know that *LQ* and *EQ* refer to "likability quotient" and "emotional quotient." Although IQ certainly contributes to success, LQ and EQ factor more prominently into the behaviors of effective leaders. Most of us have encountered someone who was brilliant but who couldn't hold an intelligent conversation about matters unrelated to his or her area of expertise, or people who are so self-involved that they make thoughtless remarks that hurt the feelings of others. Your IQ is something you're born with, but your LQ and EQ determine how far it will take you—and can be developed.

This is good news for all you women who think you're not smart enough to lead. The fact is, the most effective leaders I know will never find a cure for cancer or figure out how to put a human being on Mars. They do, however, understand themselves and the people around them. Socialized to be nurturers, caretakers, and accommodators, women have learned to read subtle changes in moods, to anticipate the needs of others, and, absent formal authority, to get things done through the power of their personalities. And here's where women have the edge. Worldwide research conducted by Dr. Jean Greaves, Dr. Travis Bradberry, and Lac D. Su of TalentSmart, a global consulting firm that specializes in helping organizations develop human capital through assessments and e-learning, indicates that when it comes to IQ:

- Men and women have the same average.
- Men tend to score higher on tests of spatial ability.
- Women tend to score higher on tests of reading and verbal skills.

But if you take a look at EQ, it's a different story. Women score higher than men in overall measures of emotional intelligence, as well as in three of the four emotional intelligence skills:

- Self-management.
- Social awareness.
- Relationship management.

In the fourth category, self-awareness, women and men score equally.

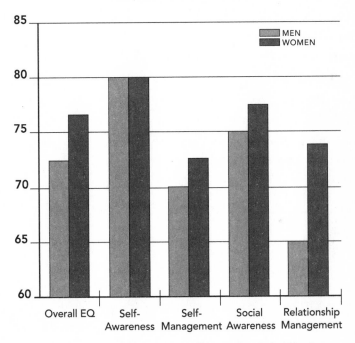

EMOTIONAL QUOTIENT:
MEN VERSUS WOMEN

Chart courtesy of Dr. Jean Greaves, Dr. Travis Bradberry, and Lac D. Su, TalentSmart.

So what does all this mean? Let me give you a quick course, beginning with emotional intelligence. Although Daniel Goleman is largely thought of as the father of emotional intelligence, many others have written about the topic. Dr. Travis Bradberry and Dr. Jean Greaves are authors of a book I like to recommend: *The Emotional Intelligence Quick Book: Everything You Need to Know to Put Your EQ to Work.* One reason I like their book is that it includes a password where you can go online and take a free emotional intelligence test. It's also thoroughly readable and directly applicable to how you lead. Along with singling out the four key components to emotional intelligence noted above, they divide these into two skills: personal competence and social competence. The following chart may help you better understand the concept:

COMPETENCE SKILLS

	WHAT I SEE	WHAT I DO
PERSONAL COMPETENCE	Your ability to accurately perceive your own emotions, and stay aware of them as they happen. This includes keeping on top of how you tend to respond to specific situations and people.	Your ability to use awareness of your emotions to stay flexible and positively direct your behavior. This means managing your emotional reactions to all situations and people.
SOCIAL COMPETENCE	Your ability to accurately pick up on emotions in other people and understand what is really going on. This often means understanding what other people are thinking and feeling even if you don't feel the same way.	Your ability to use awareness of your own emotions and the emotions of others to manage interactions successfully. This ensures clear communications and effective handling of conflict.

Chart courtesy of Dr. Travis Bradberry and Dr. Jean Greaves, TalentSmart.

People often ask me if these behaviors can be learned. I absolutely believe that they can. But it's a little like the old joke about how many psychologists it takes to change a lightbulb: *It only takes one, but the lightbulb has to really* want *to change.* It's the same for leaders. I've worked with leaders at all levels of corporations and nonprofit organizations and found that those who are the most likely to change possess these characteristics coming into the coaching engagement:

FACTORS CRITICAL TO DEVELOPING EMOTIONAL INTELLIGENCE

Factor	Described As
1. Desire	Sees the value in developing skills complementary to existing strengths.
2. Insight	When presented with concrete feedback, can see him- or herself as others do.
3. Candor	Can openly and honestly discuss development areas.
4. Openness	Shifts paradigms—does not get stuck in what worked in the past.
5. Risk taking	Is able to engage in new, uncomfortable, and what may be perceived as potentially risky new behavior.
6. A "learning" attitude	Likes to read, experience, or learn for the sake of learning, not because it's ultimately practical or utilitarian.
7. Humility	Understands that he or she is human and there's always room to grow.
8. Emotional health	Is free from or in treatment for problems such as alcoholism, drug abuse, obsessive-compulsive behavior, bipolar disease, etc.

If you want to know if *you* can increase your emotional intelligence, assess the degree to which each of the above factors is true of you. The more that are true, the easier it will be for you to develop the skills needed to lead.

SELF-AWARENESS AND SELF-MANAGEMENT:
THE INWARD FOCUS

Being able to assess your feelings at any given moment *and* use that knowledge to regulate your emotions is critical to securing the trust and confidence of your followers or those you want to influence. Let me share a story with you about a woman I coached who wasn't self-aware and how it played out in her everyday behaviors. Sybil was the executive director of a large nonprofit agency headquartered in Chicago. She was responsible for overseeing a staff of 150 people with an annual budget of $9.5 million. I was contacted by her board of directors because they felt she wasn't effectively leading the agency. It wasn't that she wasn't smart or didn't possess the technical skills needed to do the job; she was, and she did. The problem was that she would ridicule staff in front of their peers, was prone to angry outbursts, and generally created an atmosphere of fear and intimidation.

When I met with Sybil for the first time, I was impressed with her professional appearance, her ability to articulate her thoughts clearly and succinctly, and the swiftness with which she analyzed questions and responded on multiple levels. In other words, she had the look, sound, and thought processes of a leader. These factors were probably what landed her the job in the first place—they were necessary for her role, but not sufficient to lead in this particular organizational culture. When we talked about the feedback I had gotten from her board, she was quick to downplay it and cast blame on the board members themselves. She described them as a bunch of "bleeding hearts who never ran a business of this size and are more concerned with making sure everyone is happy than ensuring they do their jobs properly." When I asked if there was any truth to the comment that she publicly demeaned others, her response was, "Half of them shouldn't be here to begin with and the other half are just thin-skinned. I'm not paid to mollycoddle them. I'm paid to run a business."

As I usually do in initial coaching sessions, I asked Sybil about her background and the path that had brought her to this role. She told me she'd grown up in a military family that moved quite a bit throughout her childhood. Her dad was a four-star general (and also an alcoholic) who ran the household with an iron fist. When I remarked that this must have been somewhat frightening for a little girl, she denied it. "It built character," she said. She learned early on that discipline and hard work were the keys to success. When I asked if moving around so much was difficult, she said no. She enjoyed moving from place to place where she could get to know new people and new cultures. And when I asked if she remained in contact with any of her childhood or college friends, she couldn't recall any.

In between this first coaching session and the second, I solicited feedback from her staff about how they viewed her leadership style. This served only to confirm what the board had already told me, but it did provide concrete data with which to hold up the mirror to Sybil. When I met with her to review the feedback report, she laughed at some of the comments more sensitive leaders might cringe at and reiterated that her staff consisted essentially of underperformers who resisted her efforts to lead them. Then I probed into this notion of everyone being underperformers. She went on to explain how she couldn't stand people who weren't smart and that she had inherited a lot of those kinds of people on her staff. When I suggested that this disdain for people must be leaking out to them and causing them to feel inferior, she denied it. She might not suffer fools gladly, she told me, but she treated everyone with respect.

By now I think you've gotten the picture. Based on the coaching model that I developed and wrote about in my book *Stop Sabotaging Your Career: 8 Proven Strategies to Succeed—In Spite of Yourself,* our greatest strengths are developed early in childhood, and our development areas are typically related to the failure to build complementary skills. It was clear to me that Sybil was cut off from her feelings and those of others. I just couldn't buy that a little girl would find it quite so easy to cope with what went on in her household when she was a child. I believe that her survival from a young age depended on developing the defense mechanism of denying that anything could possibly be wrong—and that she continued to use it to the point that it had now become a blind spot for her. This was a lightbulb that wasn't going to change. My best efforts at trying to build a trusting relationship with her in which she might feel safe exploring some of the behaviors that were about to derail her were not successful. I don't think it was that she didn't *want* to be a good leader; I think she *couldn't* let go of the walls that had protected her for so long. This inability ultimately led to her termination after only eighteen months on the job.

Fortunately, I don't encounter many people like this in my coaching practice. Perhaps 10 to 15 percent of my clients are incapable of enhancing their self-awareness and self-management skills. What they all tend to have in common is over-reliance on skills developed early in childhood—to the exclusion of developing complementary behaviors. The vast majority of the clients I work with exhibit a normal degree of resistance to change in the beginning of the coaching process, then realize that perception is reality. *We are judged not by our intentions, but by our actions—and our actions are shaped by our feelings and emotions.* That's why it's so important to be able to assess and monitor them before they become impediments to leading.

Developing Your Self-Awareness and Self-Management EQ

The term *acting out* is often applied to children, but adults act out, too. What it really means is not being in touch with how you feel, or not being able to express it, and therefore you act out those feelings. Many times women will cry at work when they're angry because they've been socialized to avoid expressions of anger. They are typically not even aware they're angry. That's a form of acting out. Self-awareness and self-management require constant vigilance on your part. Here are a few exercises to help you develop increased skill in these two areas of emotional intelligence:

- **Regularly ask yourself, *What am I feeling in this moment?*** This will help you increase your awareness of your feelings and develop a vocabulary to describe them. If while you're sitting in a meeting, you ask yourself that question and answer *Frustrated,* think about what's causing it and what you can do to shift that dynamic. If you're frustrated, chances are others feel the same way. Before yelling at your child because he disobeyed you, ask the question. If you answer *Angry,* share that feeling rather than acting it out. When you feel tears beginning to well up, ask the question. If you answer *Sad,* stay with the feeling and more deeply explore what's making you sad. Being in touch with your feelings decreases the likelihood that you will act them out in counterproductive ways.

- **Keep a journal:** Many people are better at externalizing words than simply having them rummage around in their mind. A journal can help you track your feelings over time and assist you with discovering patterns of which you may not be aware. A small notepad or tape recorder in your purse or briefcase is enough to do the trick.

- **Exercise:** There's a reason so many male executives spend time on the treadmill or at the gym. They know that in addition to keeping them physically fit, the exercise contributes to their emotional well-being. Riding a bike, playing tennis, or any other activity that enables endorphins to be released can help you keep your moods and emotions in perspective and reduce the likelihood of angry, stress-related outbursts.

SOCIAL AWARENESS AND RELATIONSHIP MANAGEMENT: THE OUTWARD FOCUS

These are areas in which I believe women excel. From an early age, we are expected to conform to certain social protocols (think coming-out, sweet sixteen, or *quinceañero* parties), and it is on our shoulders that the responsibility for managing family, social, and professional relationships often falls. Think about it. Is it you or your husband who's more likely to notice that the hosts of a party are tired and it's time to go? Who can tell when the baby is about to have a meltdown? To do this effectively requires what author Anne Morrow Lindbergh called "surrendering" to the moment. What gets in the way of being effective at it is typically a preoccupation with your own thoughts or problems, needing to be right all the time, wanting to control the situation, or thinking you already know how the other person feels or what she wants to say. Sound like anyone you know?

How many times have you asked a friend "Is something wrong?" or remarked to your partner that he seems a million miles away? These behaviors are related to social awareness—the ability to pick up on verbal and nonverbal cues that often communicate even more loudly than words. When you choose not to bring up a difficult topic because you don't feel the timing is right, you're exhibiting relationship management—using your powers of perception to approach or avoid subjects as the situation dictates. My coaching client Sybil was not only unaware of her own feelings but also oblivious to the responses and feelings of others. She couldn't see when she had offended someone, which resulted in damage to the leader-follower relationship and her ability to build meaningful relationships with others. Chiyo Maniwa, on the other hand, is a different story.

I met Chiyo about a decade ago when I was doing a team-building program for an executive staff of which she was a member. From the beginning, she stood out from the group in terms of her ability to articulate her own opinions and simultaneously assimilate those of others. She could read the emotions of the group and help resolve the conflicts that naturally come up when strongminded people with diverse opinions get together.

We stayed in touch over the years, and as I got to know her I learned that her leadership path began at the University of California–Berkeley in the late 1960s. She participated in the Third World Strike to give a voice to students of color that ultimately led to the creation of an ethnic studies program, which has since become institutionalized. She's held many leadership positions subsequently, including the one she had when I met her, director of Project NATEEN, an off-site program sponsored by Children's Hospital Los Angeles that provides pregnant and parenting teens with peer counseling and case management for a full spectrum of health care, education, and counseling for themselves and their children.

Because of the challenges inherent to working with teens, the NATEEN staff was young (some teenagers themselves) and consisted primarily of African American and Latino employees. They were your typical Generation X and Y workers. Chiyo's success was largely due to her own social awareness and ability to manage relationships. Here's how she did it:

My challenge leading this group was that I really came from a totally different mind-set—a totally different paradigm. I always held positions where I led more informally. When I assumed the leadership at NATEEN, I was suddenly "management" and was viewed as an adversary. My whole history was one of political and social change where everyone was working together to achieve the same goal. I had to release judgment about who I was working with and what motivated them, and work with the reality of what I had.

Learning to connect and work with Generations X and Y was so different than when I first started working in social service. They were very much about What have you done for me? *and I was about* What can I do for you or the community? *It wasn't just a matter of accepting them, but of growing in my own way of looking at things and allowing them to provide forward thinking in areas I may have been stuck. I learned that I had to do a lot of appreciating before I could give them feedback. I also learned that motivating today's workforce is a balancing act—being too*

liberal or flexible didn't work, but neither did just being direc-
tive. This generation wants both flexibility and guidance. I had
to learn not to be reactive, even in an organization where crises
were the norm. There's a lot of work leaders have to do on them-
selves before they can lead others.

Without knowing it, Chiyo exhibited superior emotional intelligence by adapting her leadership style and expectations to meet
the needs of her followers. Like many of the other women interviewed for this book, she is guided by a well-defined set of values
(in this case, to be of service to others), uses these to build strong
relationships that help her achieve organizational goals, and isn't
afraid to admit when there's something she's got to learn to be
even better at what she does.

Developing Your Social Awareness and Relationship Management EQ

Although women tend to score higher than men at both these
components of emotional intelligence, they frequently misread
neutral cues as being negative or critical. In this regard, developing skills in social awareness and relationship management isn't
so much about doing it *more,* but rather doing it more *accurately.*
Absent information to the contrary, women are likely to ascribe
negative intent to silence. Given how much silence we get from our
male counterparts, that's a lot of negativity!

Awareness of your own feelings is really the place to start being
a better and more objective observer and synthesizer of the feelings
of others. This will prevent you from projecting your feelings onto
others or into situations where these feelings don't really exist. Once
you've got that under your belt, try some of these suggestions:

- **Ask more questions:** Many times we make erroneous assumptions about how people feel. If you notice someone sitting with a grimace on his face, don't assume he's angry or upset. That's what it looks like when some people are *thinking*. If you're not sure what nonverbal language means, ask.

- **Reflect feelings:** This technique of active listening is designed to help you and the other person more deeply understand the emotional content of spoken messages. For example, if your child's teacher says, "I've repeatedly told your son not to disrupt the rest of the class when his work is completed, yet he continues to do so," a reflection would be, "It seems like you're feeling pretty frustrated with his lack of responsiveness to your requests." It doesn't matter if you're on target; if you're not, the other person will respond with what he or she really *is* feeling. In this case, the teacher may say something like, "It's not really frustration, it's more concern that he's not being respectful of the other students. This is something he needs to learn." Now you've got a more accurate idea of what she's feeling and you can respond appropriately.

- **Be willing to share your own feelings and express your needs:** Remaining tuned in to others but not factoring in your own needs isn't leadership. In the real world, there's a give-and-take that can require problem solving to ensure everyone's needs are heard and (hopefully) met. Just because you understand why someone made a mistake doesn't mean you have to tolerate that same mistake over and over again. Once you understand where people are coming from and how they feel about the situation, you can build a bridge to your emotional experience and what you'd like to see happen. It might sound like this: "I understand what you're saying and the frustration you're feeling about not getting the promotion you think you deserved. If I were in your situation, I might feel the same way. I see it a little differently, though, and I'd like to give you some feedback that will help you to get on track for a promotion in the future."

LQ: LIKABILITY QUOTIENT

The coaches in my office have developed a very scientific test for measuring likability. It's called "the beer test." When we first meet someone, we decide whether we would like to go out and have a beer or a cup of coffee with the person. If the answer's yes, he or she passes the likability test. If the answer's no, we know we have our work cut out for us. For a while now, I've wanted to design an inventory to measure likability. The problem is, individuals differ with respect to the kinds of people they gravitate toward, and *likability* means different things to different people. There is no one way or right way of being likable, but likable people share some common traits:

- Go out of their way to make others feel comfortable in their presence.
- Exhibit a genuine interest in others.
- Have learned the art of listening.
- Smile at people.
- Are consistent in their temperament.
- Are empathetic.
- Draw people toward them.
- Are sensitive to the feelings of others.
- Look for ways to build bridges of common understanding.

When it comes to likability, however, women often go to an extreme. You might be old enough to remember the acceptance speech Sally Field gave a number of years ago for her Academy Award–winning performance in the film *Places in the Heart:* "You like me, you really like me!" she gushed from the podium. As if she needed an Oscar to validate her likability. There's a spectrum of likability that goes from an inordinate need to be liked to not caring how others perceive you.

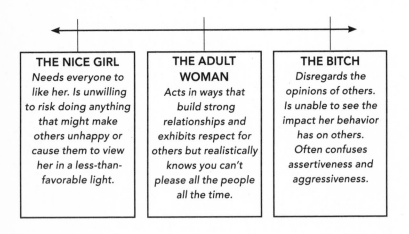

THE NICE GIRL	THE ADULT WOMAN	THE BITCH
Needs everyone to like her. Is unwilling to risk doing anything that might make others unhappy or cause them to view her in a less-than-favorable light.	*Acts in ways that build strong relationships and exhibits respect for others but realistically knows you can't please all the people all the time.*	*Disregards the opinions of others. Is unable to see the impact her behavior has on others. Often confuses assertiveness and aggressiveness.*

In his book *The Likeability Factor,* Tim Sanders provides some tangible reasons why you want to brush up on your likability:

- Doctors give more time to patients they like and less to those they don't.
- A positively charged work environment produces superior profits due to reduced turnover and increased customer satisfaction.
- Success in the workplace is most influenced not by what or whom you know, but by your popularity.

- People—unlike animals—gain success not by being aggressive, but by being nice. The most successful leaders (from CEOs to PTA presidents) treat people with respect and make genuine attempts to be liked.
- In the legal world, if your client is a likable person, it will affect the compensation a jury awards to him or her.
- Recent studies regarding marriage and divorce indicate that one of the primary elements of marital success is likability. Easygoing, likable people have half the divorce rate of the general population, and when both parties are congenial, the risk of divorce is reduced by an additional 50 percent.

When it comes to leadership, likable leaders tend to gain the cooperation and goodwill of those upon whom they depend to get the job done. That's why I cringe when I hear a leader say, "I'm not here to win a popularity contest." My response is always, "Oh, yes you are." You can increase your likability by doing a few simple things:

- Learn the names of the people in your company or on your floor—even if you don't interact regularly with them or need anything from them.
- Smile at people when you walk by them in the hall.
- When people talk to you, stop whatever you're doing, shift your focus, and listen to them.
- Remember what people say to you and follow up by asking questions.
- Avoid jokes and remarks that could be even remotely offensive.
- Laugh at yourself.
- Admit your mistakes—be human, not perfect.

POLITICAL SAVVY: A UNIQUE FORM OF EMOTIONAL INTELLIGENCE

While writing this book, I had to take a break for a surgical procedure. My surgeon was a gifted woman, but her administrative staff left something to be desired. They couldn't seem to coordinate all the diagnostic and surgical procedures in a timely fashion, didn't call me until the day before the surgery to let me know about it, and forgot to call the hospital to arrange the ancillary services required, so that when I was wheeled into radiology they were not prepared. Fortunately for me, I have a neighbor who understands politics in the workplace and works at the same hospital; she was able to run interference for me. She used her political skills to get me the same anesthesiologist she would want if she were having surgery. When she heard they were going to send me home because they didn't have everything they needed for the procedure, she used her political skills to get what was required. When I mentioned that a particular specialist I wanted to see couldn't fit me in for several weeks because he was so busy, she called him and used her political skills to get me in the next day. Why, then, do women think of politics in the workplace as smarmy or unseemly? They avoid it like a three-scoop ice cream sundae with hot fudge and whipped cream (maybe even more).

When it comes right down to it, politics (whether it's in Washington, your local hospital, or the workplace) is nothing more than the business of relationships—and that's something women are downright good at! Being adept at politics helps you to get your job done with the maximum cooperation and least muscle needed to be effective. Author Kathleen Kelley Reardon has her finger on the pulse of workplace politics and writes extensively about it. Her work in this arena is so thorough and on-target that I urge you to read her two books *The Secret Handshake: Mastering the Politics of the Business Inner Circle* and *It's All Politics: Winning in a World Where Hard Work and Talent Aren't Enough.* Both are great reads filled with practical advice, including the following suggestions for how you can build "relationships the politically savvy way."

Know What Others Need and Want—and Let Them Know When You Provide It

I've already discussed the importance of being a good observer of human behavior. This comes in particularly handy when it comes to learning what's important to other people and delivering value-added products or services. But knowing and delivering aren't where it ends. Too many women assume others will *notice* when they've gone out of their way to get a job done or done it with particular precision and skill. "People are far too busy to follow or be aware of your accomplishments," says Reardon. "You have to let them know. The key here is to be strategic in telling them. Choose the right method and the right time." One way you can do this is to factually inform management of your achievements. For example, rather than simply say a particular project was completed, you might say, "I'm proud to report my team completed the Crenshaw project two weeks ahead of schedule and 15 percent under budget." As a friend of mine says, "If you don't blow your own horn, no one will know you're in the band."

Manage Reciprocity

I frequently talk about the quid pro quo that's inherent to every relationship—that is, the constant exchange of favors, assistance, information, friendship, and so on. If you're not mentally keeping track of it, you're making a mistake, but not because you may not be getting your fair share of the bargain; it's because you may not be *giving* enough in the exchange to begin with. In Reardon's words, "Asking someone you've never bothered to establish a relationship with for a favor . . . is a form of political fumbling. She doesn't know whether you'll ever return the favor since she doesn't know your track record. She doesn't owe you anything and hasn't the foggiest idea what you'll ever be able to do for her." If you've read any of my other books or heard me speak, you know this is a point with which I could not agree more. In my words: *When you need a relationship, it's too late to build it.*

Develop Your Favor Bank

You may ask yourself what you have to offer as a favor. Believe me, there are plenty of favors being exchanged all the time—some more obvious than others. I love to tell the story of the woman who, for several years, asked me for assistance with writing an affirmative action plan for her department. These are cumbersome documents to prepare, but each year I did so with the knowledge that I had the expertise and was happy to help her. Several years after the last time I helped her, we had both moved on—me to start my own consulting firm, and her to another department of the company where we both initially worked. One day the phone rang, and it was her. She had a colleague coming in from Indonesia who was looking to meet American consultants for the purpose of bringing them to her country for projects based there, and she wanted to know if I'd like to meet the woman. Making a very long story short, that was more than twenty years ago and I still go to Indonesia several times a year to work on consulting projects. The moral of the story is: *You never know how doing a favor for someone is going to benefit you.*

Surprise People with Unexpected Favors

Reardon points out that unexpected favors aren't always the obvious. "If a person did you a favor by meeting with you, an immediate thank-you note is effective. If, however, the person has only spoken with you in passing, the impact of a personal note recalling something he said might be greater if you send it a month after you met. That you remember his interests so long after parting company indicates that you were really listening to him and that he's remained on your mind."

Show Gratitude Consistent with What You Received

When it comes to favors, I do them willingly for others and rarely expect anything in return. I know that the universe will reward me appropriately when I least expect and most need it. That's why I'm surprised I remember an incident from many years ago that bugs me to this day—but it does speak to the importance of proper gratitude. A corporate client of mine wanted to add a component of workplace communication to a training program we conducted quarterly in countries around the world. Not only was it a lucrative piece of business, but it was also fun—we stayed at the best accommodations in exotic locations paid for by a firm that treated its outside consultants quite well. I recommended a colleague of mine for the work, and he landed the contract for this project as well as several others in the company over a period of years. One year he sent me a "chocolate pizza" with no personal note as his thanks. As much as I appreciated his thoughtfulness, it just didn't match the magnitude of the favor. A personal note indicating appreciation for the confidence I placed in him through the referral would have meant so much more. A referral to one of his clients would have been even better!

Give Credit Even When It Isn't Due

I'm sure your mother, like mine, had a little saying for nearly every life lesson. Remember *You catch more flies with honey than you do with vinegar*? Well, that's what this suggestion is all about. Letting people save face and reinforcing even small points of agreement goes a long way toward building politically effective relationships—and it doesn't cost you a dime. Rather than looking for the point of *disagreement* in what others are saying, look for the point with which you can specifically and genuinely *agree* as a means of giving them credit. Here are some examples:

- I like what you're saying about the need to investigate other options. I was focusing on the way we've always done it. Let's see how we can take the best of both.

- Thank you for collecting all of this information in advance. It's helped me to see what we still need, so let me give you a little more direction for how to fill in the blanks.

- Your attention to detail is so much better than mine. Now let's take a look at how we can connect the dots to reach the right conclusion.

Make Connections

Unlike actually building relationships, making connections means simply getting on the other person's radar screen. You've read several stories so far in this book (and have yet to read a few others) that came from making connections at events I've attended. It isn't that I don't enjoy or I'm not cordial to everyone I come into contact with, but when I meet certain people and I know they have a message to communicate, I'm certain to get their contact information and ask if I might call them in the future. This is making a connection. Sometimes those connections do turn into relationships, but most don't. "The more sophisticated organizational politicians don't haphazardly fling their cards at complete strangers. They seem to have a kind of radar that tells them whom they should seek out. This radar comes from having done their homework. A true mover and shaker works the room—any room—intelligently," explains Reardon.

Play It Closer to the Vest

Poker players know that you should hold your cards close to your vest if you don't want other players to be able to see them before they're played. In the name of fairness, women often think they need to share *everything* they know about a subject or every piece of information that may have been given to them about a project. Nothing could be further from the truth. Knowledge is power, and there are times when keeping all or some of it to yourself is the best course of action. Here's one place that women really need to heed Reardon's sage advice: "You have to know whom to trust with information. Friendship complicates things because it brings with it certain obligations to share information. So the fewer you have of them at work, the less you'll feel pressured to spill the beans when you should be keeping information to yourself." Does this mean as a leader you should isolate yourself? Absolutely not! Look at how men build close professional relationships without ever calling them "friendships." This is something a woman does. You need information coming to you at all times, but you need to manage the reciprocal aspect of it. One suggestion Reardon makes for dealing with people who try to provoke you to disclose information is to use "apparent self-disclosure." This means sharing information that may be new to the person but is actually not risky for you and usually discoverable with a little digging.

Coaching Tips for Enhancing Your LQ And EQ

61. **Read The Emotional Intelligence Quick Book.** It really is just that—a quick guide to learning more about EQ. It also provides you with the opportunity to assess your own EQ, which is a good place to start identifying your developmental needs in this arena.

62. **Solicit 360-degree feedback.** There really is no better way to have the mirror held up so that you can see yourself as others see you. Asking three simple questions will yield a wealth of information—usually about behaviors related to emotional intelligence: What do I do well that I should continue doing? What can I do more of to be even more effective? What can I do less of to be even more effective? As with any kind of feedback or survey, be prepared to take action.

63. **Approach leadership as a discipline to be learned.** This means reading books about leadership, attending workshops, and subscribing to magazines geared toward leaders. Becoming an expert on leadership will make you feel more confident in your abilities and reduce the likelihood of acting out your insecurities.

64. **Stop being a human doing and start being a human being.** If you can't suspend the compulsion to *do*, you can't understand how you or others *feel*. Workaholics and other compulsive doers often use those behaviors to avoid painful or unpleasant feelings. An essential component of emotional intelligence is the ability to empathize—and empathy begins at home. If this sounds like you, try sitting quietly for five min-

utes with no music, television, or other distractions. Focus on your breathing and see what feelings pop up. Then deal with those using self-help books, therapy, or, if necessary, anti-anxiety medication.

65. **Read** It's All Politics: Winning in a World Where Hard Work and Talent Aren't Enough. Kathleen Kelley Reardon brilliantly dissects the meaning of workplace politics and offers practical ways to excel at it. Her refreshing perspective will help you overcome your hesitance about being better at politics.

66. *Lead with questions—particularly if you tend to be critical.* Rather than point out what's wrong about someone's idea, make the first thing out of your mouth a question so that you can at least understand the other person's rationale. Then follow up with a point of agreement that prefaces your own viewpoint.

67. *Exercise your empathy muscle.* Rather than simply acknowledge that you've heard the message when someone shares something with you that's painful, respond from the heart. Say something like "That must be really hard for you" or "I'm so sorry to hear about that." It's better to err on the side of being too empathic rather than not being empathic enough.

68. *Surrender to the moment.* Emotionally intelligent people know when to let go of their own agenda to meet someone else's. That means you are able to momentarily put aside your need to speak in favor of enabling yourself to listen.

69. *Attend NTL's Interpersonal Skills for Leadership Success workshop.* NTL (National Training Laboratory; http://ntl .org) is this country's premier provider of experiential training programs. Its four-day program teaches you the interpersonal

and influence skills needed to achieve business goals through self-awareness and enhanced interpersonal communication techniques.

70. ***Treat everyone with whom you come into contact with unconditional positive regard.*** There's a scene from the movie *The War* where Kevin Costner gives the neighborhood bullies some cotton candy he had just bought for his own children. When his kids ask him why, he replies, "Because it looks like they ain't been given nothin' for a long time." That's unconditional positive regard. From the doorman to the CEO, whether or not you think someone can do something for you, and whether someone shares your values and viewpoints or is diametrically opposed to them, treat people not like you would want to be treated, but like you would want your mother, spouse, child, or best friend to be treated.

71. ***Always allow others to save face.*** There is *never* a need to embarrass someone in front of others, or to act in ways that diminish another's self-esteem or damage the relationship. Even when you're at your most angry (especially when), your comments should be tough on the problem, gentle on the person. It's not a sign of weakness. Others won't take advantage of you. It's the emotionally intelligent thing to do.

72. ***Collect more chips for your political account than you can possibly ever use.*** Do favors, offer genuine praise, provide support, learn what's important to people, and give it to them.

CHAPTER EIGHT

Women as Entrepreneurs: Leading Your Own Enterprise

I ran the wrong kind of business, but I did it with integrity.
—Sydney Biddle Barrows (the Mayflower Madam)

You've already been an entrepreneur if you've:

- Had a lemonade stand.
- Sold Girl Scout cookies.
- Designed a fund-raiser for a nonprofit organization.
- Developed a new product or system for your employer.
- Ran a department within a large organization.

I realize that not everyone wants to be an entrepreneur, but some of you reading this book may be leading your own non-profit organization or business—either large or small. Then again, some of you may *want* to start your own business or non-profit but aren't sure of your entrepreneurial capabilities. In either case, the leadership tips that have been provided thus far will be useful to you in various aspects of your daily work. The self-assessment on the next page will help you gauge your entrepreneurial temperament. Whether you aspire to leading your own enterprise or getting better at leading one you don't own, the success stories in this chapter will be of interest to you, beginning with a woman who has made a lot of dough in the past thirty years.

Debbi Fields, best known for her Mrs. Fields Cookies, is one of the most successful and high-profile women entrepreneurs alive. Inducted into the National Society of Entrepreneurs in 2003, Debbi was an unlikely success story. She had no credentials, business experience, or college education, but she knew she made great cookies and had a passion for doing so. Everyone was convinced she was never going to make anything of herself, so she set out to prove them wrong. In 1977, she convinced a bank to loan her money for what many thought was a losing proposition from the outset. With her motto *Good enough never is,* she proved the naysayers wrong by creating an empire worth $450 million with sixteen hundred international locations.

Most of us will never be entrepreneurs on a par with Debbi Fields, but many of us are successful entrepreneurs doing what we love and making money in the process. I want to share the stories of five very different women who started enterprises equally successful, if not quite so large. Before I do, why don't you take a moment to complete the following self-assessment. It will help you to determine if your entrepreneurial leanings go in the right direction.

ENTREPRENEURIAL ASSESSMENT

Answer each of the following questions *true, false,* or *sometimes.*

_____ 1. I view obstacles as challenges to overcome.

_____ 2. When working on a project that intrigues me, I lose track of time.

_____ 3. I am goal-oriented.

_____ 4. I rarely make the same mistake twice.

_____ 5. If I say I'm going to do something, it gets done.

_____ 6. Success is important to me.

_____ 7. I'm often the one to come up with new ideas or new ways to do things.

_____ 8. Change doesn't bother me.

_____ 9. I like learning new things—even things I see no immediate use for.

_____ 10. I trust my intuition.

_____ 11. When told something is impossible, I try even harder.

_____ 12. I'll work doggedly on a problem until it's solved.

_____ 13. I take calculated risks.

_____ 14. I don't suffer from analysis paralysis.

_____ 15. I like to travel to new and exotic places.

_____ 16. I bounce back quickly from setbacks.

_____ 17. I'm self-confident.

_____ 18. I see the glass as half full.

_____ 19. I view mistakes as inevitable.

_____ 20. I'm willing to give up security in the present for possible long-term rewards.

_____ 21. I prefer to travel the road less taken.

_____ 22. I make decisions based on having _enough_ information, not _all_ the information.

_____ 23. I enjoy working independently.

_____ 24. I like to lead projects and people.

_____ 25. _Persistent_ is my middle name.

Scoring

3 for each *True* answer

2 for each *Sometimes* answer

0 for each *False* answer

60–75	You not only can but *should* have your own business. Start thinking about and planning for what you would most love to be doing with your life.
48–59	There's definite potential, but take a look at those areas where you answered *false* or *sometimes* and focus on what you need to do to ensure success.
37–47	The desire is there, but the skill level may not be. You're going to have to push yourself in areas outside your comfort zone or perhaps partner with others who can complement your natural skills.
Below 37	Unless you have some overwhelming desire to start your own enterprise or can contribute to an entrepreneurship in a narrowly defined area of expertise, you may be better off employed by someone else.

IT'S THAT VISION THING AGAIN

Perhaps the characteristic that most differentiates entrepreneurial leaders from those who choose to work for someone else is the entrepreneur's vision. When you work for someone else, the overarching vision is already there. Whether it's to build homes, provide legal services, or give away money through a community foundation, there's a vision that precedes building the business—

and it usually comes from an entrepreneur! I'm always surprised at the number of people who tell me they want to start a business of some kind but don't know what they would like it to be. True entrepreneurs already have a vision for what they want to do to make money, improve society, create a product, or enhance their own lives. It's a driving force that impels them to go out and make their vision a reality. It would be pretty difficult to be a successful entrepreneur without a vision.

When I was first introduced to Katherine Chon at a keynote event, I had no clue she would be someone I would eventually write about. She's young, small, unassuming, and polite to a fault. When a group of us were going to the hotel bar for a drink, I asked if she was going to join us. She said, "If you invite me, I will." Of course I later just had to coach her that she didn't need an invitation to join a group; she should have assumed she was welcome simply by my question. Which goes to show that leaders come in all kinds of packages.

Katherine cofounded and is currently co–executive director for the Polaris Project, headquartered in Washington, DC. The mission of the Polaris Project is to combat human trafficking and modern-day slavery. Just to show how ignorant I was, I thought this kind of thing happened somewhere else—not in *our* country. In fact, statistics show that 365 nights of the year, there are girls as young as twelve working as sex slaves, forced to have sex with ten to fifteen men in order to meet a nightly quota of five hundred to a thousand dollars—none of which they keep. There are an estimated 27 million people in modern-day slavery across the world, some in the sex trade, some used for other purposes. Of those, 17,500 are brought into the United States for this purpose every year.

The summer before her senior year at Brown University, Katherine lived in an apartment building with other students, and each night they got together to talk about social issues. One night the subject of modern-day slavery came up. Katherine was shocked to learn it still existed. As is the case with many entrepreneurs, there is a moment of inspiration from which the vision is born. This particular night was that moment for Katherine:

> *The conversation got me curious, so I went online and Googled "human trafficking." I learned it's the third largest and fastest-growing criminal industry in the world, victimizing millions of people. . . . I continued to learn about the issue and found I couldn't turn my back on it. The day after graduation we had a U-Haul packed up and drove to Washington, DC. We didn't know where we would go or where the funding would come from, but we knew we wanted to build what is now called Polaris Project from the ground up.*
>
> *We chose Washington because that's where the agencies were based and we wanted to do some kind of policy work. We quickly realized that Polaris as a grassroots agency was filling a gap in the anti-trafficking movement. At first I was intimidated by the authority and power on Capitol Hill that comes with age and life experience. Now we're one of the only agencies that work with all different kinds of trafficking—foreign nationals, American women and children, sex trafficking, labor trafficking. Most agencies focus on just one population. We have a comprehensive strategy. Our direct service work helps us to advocate for stronger policies as well as for the victims and survivors. The criminal networks adapt quickly to change and the governments don't, so there's an imbalance to our efforts. We are able to adapt quickly*

*and don't fear change. I realize it took over a hundred years to
abolish slavery in the US, so it's going to be a long haul.*

*There's never been a time when I think I should never have
done this. The tagline for Polaris is* Imagine freedom, *and it
means something to me personally. I never pictured myself as an
entrepreneur, but I really enjoy having the freedom to do what I
love. I wake up excited to come to work. Putting in hundred-hour
weeks doesn't bother me. To be able to live life in that way and be
happy and fulfilled and at the end of the day know I make an impact is something I could never regret. It's opened my eyes to what
freedom really is and how people can experience it. It's like in* The
Matrix—*once you choose to take the pill, you can't really go back.*

Like many entrepreneurs, Katherine started with passion for a
cause and jumped in feetfirst. She learned by doing. She identified
a need and met it. She became an expert in her field not through
her college education, but through learning and immersing herself
in the topic of human trafficking. Katherine also influences others
from a strong knowledge base. Not being bound by an organizational structure that dictates what she can and can't do, she forges
new ground every day. She has a strategic plan but is smart enough
to know that it has to be flexible and meet emerging needs. Never
having read a book on leadership, she now coleads an organization
that's making a difference in the world. How many of us would like
to be able to say the same?

Entrepreneurial Lessons

- Even if your vision isn't crystal clear when you start, it will
  drive your direction and eventually come into focus.
- Vision alone isn't enough. Develop a strategy to achieve it.

- Passion is essential for the entrepreneur to put in the number of hours and amount of energy needed to succeed.
- Immerse yourself in learning about all facets of your enterprise—become the expert to whom others turn.
- Don't let the competition discourage you—you can distinguish yourself by providing better, faster, or more customer-centered service.
- Your enterprise has to complement your values.

SEIZING A GOOD OPPORTUNITY

One night as I was driving from Los Angeles to Palm Springs, I saw a billboard in the middle of a desert stretch of Interstate 10 that read: THERE IS NO GREATER BURDEN THAN A GOOD OPPORTUNITY. It said nothing else, and I never saw the sign again—which made me wonder if this was a *Twilight Zone* moment meant to send a message to only me. If so, it worked, because I never forgot it. Every once in a while a great opportunity presents itself, and you have to decide whether you're willing to take the chance of going for it or spending the rest of your life wondering if you should have. Personally, I'm one of those people who would prefer to take the chance and learn from it regardless of how it turns out. In fact, for nearly twenty years I've had a hand-carved wooden sign in my office that I bought in Bali; it reads: NO GUTS, NO GLORY. It serves as a reminder that taking risks can be scary—but it's the only way I'm going to live up to my full potential and achieve my dreams.

Not too long ago, I met a kindred spirit when I was in Chicago to give a keynote address to the local chapter of the Healthcare Businesswomen's Association. Kathy Reehling, president/CEO of CREW Technical Services, was assigned to transport me from the hotel to the speaking venue. As women often do, we chatted during the drive about our careers and our families. Warm, friendly, and unpretentious, she shared her personal story, and I was once again amazed by what women are capable of doing when presented with an opportunity too good to pass up. I also knew hers was a success story that would inspire readers by showing that a woman can create balance between family and career *and* build a multimillion-dollar business in the process!

Upon graduating from Purdue, Kathy worked for the university for six years designing databases. When her first child was born, she decided she wanted to be a stay-at-home mom—being away from her son caused her to miss "too much good stuff." A few years later, her daughter was born; by now she was spending her free time doing volunteer work, sewing, and gardening. The real turning point for Kathy was when the kids came down with chicken pox. First her son was quarantined for six weeks; then her daughter, for another six weeks. Just as cabin fever was setting in, her husband mentioned that his company, a subcontractor to the pharmaceutical company Eli Lilly, needed someone to work on 1032 databases (the same kind she'd worked on at Purdue) for a twelve-week assignment. Nearly three months of being housebound with sick children made this an appealing opportunity to Kathy. Besides, she knew she wanted to get back into the workforce at some point and figured this might be a good start.

She put on a business suit for the first time in years, found child care, and went for an interview, scared that being out of the loop for so long might have caused her to lose her competitive edge. Not only was she given the job, but by the end of the first week she realized she could do all the work assigned to her in two hours a day! So she asked for more work to fill the rest of her time with meaningful tasks rather than just stretch out the original assignment. By the end of the twelve-week contract period, Kathy was leading an entire team of people, and the company didn't want her to leave. The only problem was that the company didn't want to continue to hold the subcontract, and she didn't want to work full time for Lilly. Here's where Kathy's entrepreneurial spirit kicked in:

> *One of the men I was working with and I decided,* There's a business here, *and we got Lilly to write the contract directly with us. The first thing I did was hire my best friend to job-share with me so I could work three days a week and she would work two days a week until my daughter started first grade. Lilly kept asking for more and more people to meet their needs, and soon we realized we had a* real *company. Then one day a customer called and asked us to bid a job at Merck. That's when we realized we had to get serious and incorporate properly to make it real. I learned to do payroll and other stuff I never dreamed I would do. We were basically doing contract work for Lilly for the first four years—then these other contracts started rolling in.*
>
> *Our company policies and procedures were definitely impacted by where I was at in my own life—and contributed to our success. I knew I wanted to be there for my kids when they were young, so we developed family-friendly work policies. We recruit and retain great people because of that. We spend a lot more on our human resources than our competition, but it pays off. For example, we arrange it so that parents—and not only women—can take the whole summer off without pay but have time with their kids. If their jobs need to be covered, we hire college interns.*
>
> *The greatest challenge I had growing a business and a fam-*

ily at the same time was that no matter where I was at, I felt the pressure of the other. If I couldn't be room mother for the day, it stressed me out. Then if I was room mother and wasn't at work, it stressed me out. I realized I had to be present wherever I was, not feel guilty, and trust the people I hired. At this point we have about 120 employees and up to $28 million in gross annual revenues.

The number one piece of advice I have for women who want to become entrepreneurs is: Don't listen to the naysayers—go for it. What helped me was that I was naive about what couldn't be done. A lot of people said, "You don't want to start your own business, because you have to live, sleep, and breathe it twenty-four hours a day." If you're willing to hire good people and trust and reward them, you don't have to do that. You make it work around your own life. If you're a control freak it won't work, but otherwise it will.

What I love about Kathy's story is the fact that she seized a great opportunity when she saw it, she didn't sacrifice family for career, and she set policies consistent with her own values for how to attract and retain employees. She started her business on *her* terms, and not only did it work, it flourished. Like so many great leaders, Kathy knows what it takes to develop a loyal and motivated team of employees: simultaneously focusing on the needs of the customer and the needs of the staff.

Entrepreneurial Lessons

- Propose win-win solutions to your customers' problems. In this case, Lilly wanted Kathy, and Kathy wanted to work on her own terms. Her suggested solution put her on the path to starting her own business.

- Know when it's time to create your infrastructure. That's what Kathy meant when she said she realized they had become a "real" company and had to start acting like it. Creating your infrastructure includes developing policies and procedures, formalizing the status of your business (incorporating, becoming an LLC, what have you), filing your DBA ("doing business as"), and doing other things to protect you and your company from potential liability. Many entrepreneurs fail because they are visionaries who lack the skills or resist the need to put systems in place to support their organization's growth.

- Act in concert with your values. Kathy did this in a number of ways. First, she started her business with the knowledge that as long as her children were young, she didn't want to work full time, so she job-shared with a friend. Then, once the business grew, she knew she wanted to provide employment for people where they, too, could find work-life balance. So she developed family-friendly policies consistent with her own values.

- Set boundaries. Kathy didn't fall prey to the entrepreneur's dilemma of living and breathing the business. She was clear about what she did and didn't want, and orchestrated her business and personal life accordingly.

MAKING THE LEAP FROM EMPLOYED TO EMPLOYER

One of the biggest risks I've ever taken was to leave a full-time job to start my own business. It's one thing to complain about "working for the man"—and another to actually do something about it. Insecurities about money, identity, stability, and capability keep too many people in unfulfilling jobs for a lifetime. Someone who overcame those insecurities and made the leap is Sylvia Acevedo. I met her at the governor's mansion in Austin, Texas, prior to each of our presentations at the Texas Women's Conference. She immediately impressed me with her self-confidence, her firm handshake, and the way she looked me in the eye when we conversed. As we spoke, I learned that she's the president of CommuniCard, headquartered in Austin. I asked if I could interview her for this book, and fortunately she agreed. I had no idea what her backstory was, but I had a hunch there was one.

By the time I arrived back at my office in California, there was a package from Sylvia waiting for me. That was my first clue that she was a true entrepreneur—she doesn't let any grass grow under her feet! The package contained samples of her CommuniCards—an amazingly simple concept that makes a big difference for people trying to communicate across cultures. Each "card deck" contains common messages with pictures in a particular field, such as law enforcement, construction, or housekeeping. For example, the housekeeping deck contains a card that in both English and Spanish says WHERE ARE THE CLEANING SUPPLIES? The cards allow people to communicate efficiently with the knowledge they are being clearly understood. Sylvia thinks of them as cross-cultural bridges.

By training, Sylvia is an engineer, but at heart she's an entrepreneur. Prior to starting CommuniCard, she was a top executive with major corporations such as Dell, IBM, and Apple. Just before the technology crash in the late 1990s, Sylvia decided to take a little time off to ponder her future. She had the idea for CommuniCard brewing in her head but needed time to flesh it out. I asked her how she made the transition from working for someone else to having her own business:

> You've got to follow your passion. When you're starting a business, it's important to be grounded and do research, but even if you have a great product you must have the drive and energy that will make you want to go the extra mile when things get tough. Everything eventually gets hard, and if you don't love what you're doing, you're more likely to give up.
>
> I was able to quit my job to start my business, because I always lived below my means and made smart investments. But there are things women can do to move toward their dream of owning a business while they're still employed. Start by networking and being in lots of groups with people who aren't corporate types. Corporate people are very different from entrepreneurs, and you want to be able to learn from other entrepreneurs. Join and go to the meetings of trade associations in your industry. It's about knowing people—your network is so important. Local chambers of commerce, ethnic chambers, and women's chambers can be good, but you have to be sure they have members that will use the product or service you're going to offer. Business Network International is another group that was helpful to me. After a while you get the lay of the land.
>
> Some other things you can do while still employed are develop your business plan, create your Web site, buy your domain name, and create your press kit and marketing materials. If you do this while you're still drawing a paycheck, you can focus the first few months after you quit on sales, revenue, and working with clients.

For a long time I had a chip on my shoulder about being a Latina and thought people didn't like me because of it, but I realize now people embrace and actually look for it. Living in Austin, which is the number one city in the US for Hispanics, helps. In other cities I might not have been as successful. I've even gotten business because I'm a minority. At one time I might not have liked that, but it's something I can use to my advantage. That means you've got to be in a city that is a welcoming environment for you and your product.

Sylvia offers a lot of good tips for entrepreneurial leaders, but once again you hear that passion and leading your own enterprise go hand in hand. She's so right when she says there are inevitable hurdles to running your own business—and it's your belief in yourself and what you're doing that gets you over them. Neither Sylvia nor any of the other entrepreneurs I spoke with started their businesses with an eye on the dollar sign—they started them with passion for an idea or product. This doesn't mean they didn't do all the things required to make their endeavors financially successful, because they did. It just would have been a lot harder to jump over those inevitable hurdles if they didn't *love* what they were doing.

Something else I find helpful in Sylvia's comments are the practical tips she offers for what you can do to start moving toward your own business while you're still employed and earning a paycheck. In fact she's currently working on a card deck that breaks the process into small steps you can take over time to start your business. You might want to check her Web site—www.thecommunicard.com—to see when they're available.

Entrepreneurial Lessons

- Build your nest egg while still employed. If this means you have to live below your means, so be it. Besides, it's good practice for surviving your business's cash-flow fluctuations.

- Start networking. Go to chamber of commerce meetings after work, or join an association related to the business you want to start. Building relationships should always be a huge part of your marketing plan.

- Capitalize on what makes you different. If you're a person of color, gay or lesbian, physically challenged, or from a different country, don't be afraid to target similar people as potential clients. Register with your local small-business association as a minority- or woman-owned company.

THE AFFILIATED ENTREPRENEUR

Not all entrepreneurial leaders come up with their own ideas and start their businesses from scratch—but it doesn't make them any less successful leaders. When considering their own businesses, many women overlook opportunities to affiliate with larger brand names. Every year, there are hundreds of expos offering you opportunities to affiliate with or franchise big-name businesses. Many of these costs tens of thousands of dollars to get into, but there are those you can start out with on a much more modest budget.

Anne Newbury was a young stay-at-home mom with a four-year-old and a six-month-old infant when she visited her cousin in Dallas, Texas, one summer nearly forty years ago. They talked about Anne's interest in returning to work as a full-time school-teacher. Anne's husband had a good job, but they didn't have enough for what she described as "extras." Her cousin suggested she become a Mary Kay Independent Beauty Consultant. That suggestion changed the course of her life more than she would have imagined.

Although Mary Kay representatives work independently, they receive continuing education, guidance, recognition, and affiliation from the corporate structure. Granted, it takes a certain kind of personality to become involved with direct sales, but for someone with grit and determination, you can't beat the Mary Kay formula for success. Anne is just such a person, and as you read about how her life was transformed, keep in mind that I had to prod her to do a little bragging:

> *I've been with Mary Kay for thirty-seven years, and out of that time I have been a national sales director for thirty years. Right now I'm the number one national sales director worldwide. After my cousin suggested I check it out as a way of being able to work part time and still have time to spend with my children, I looked into it and learned the commission structure was very generous. In a very short time, I figured that I had the opportunity to make more money in one month running my own Mary Kay business part time than I could earn working full time as a teacher. It also allowed me to control the hours I worked and the amount of time I spent with my family.*
>
> *I loved what happened to me when I accomplished things and was rewarded for it. The more I accomplished, the more I wanted to do. Even now some people have said to me, "Don't you have enough money?" I can honestly say it's not about the money anymore. Once I found my journey I realized I could do more and I could help others to do more, too. As Mary Kay always said,*

*"You can't reach the top without taking other people with you."
My mother used to worry that my success meant I might have to
be away from the children too much. But I picked them up after
school, did their homework with them, and took them to the mall
or wherever else they wanted to go. My flexible schedule allowed
me to do all that. There will always be critics who might criticize
your travel schedule, your decisions, or your choosing to work
on a Saturday afternoon. I found it was a waste of my time to
be defensive because what they're really saying is "You're doing
something bigger than I think I could do."*

Anne's story serves as a lesson to every woman who wants it
all—self-esteem, independence, family, financial security, and to
make a difference. Like many women of her generation, she went
into teaching as a profession, but unlike many women of *any* generation she created and led a business within a business that allowed her to achieve goals beyond her wildest dreams. Given her
personal situation at the time, Anne probably would not have left
teaching to venture out into any kind of business that would require a large outlay of cash or require her to work alone without
an established network of procedures and colleagues. If you find
yourself in a similar situation, it could be that becoming an affiliated entrepreneur will work for you.

Entrepreneurial Lessons

- Explore entrepreneurial ventures that fit your lifestyle. If
  you have small children or a traditional marriage, a business
  that requires you to travel or work long hours probably isn't
  for you.

- Weigh the financial realities and possibilities. When Anne realized she could earn more money working part time as a Mary Kay Independent Beauty Consultant than she could working full time as a teacher, the decision to quit her teaching job wasn't too difficult.

- Be a mentor. There will come a time when your business is stable and you have more time to devote to helping others venture out on their own. Subscribe to the *Each one teach one* philosophy.

- Don't allow naysayers to shape your decisions or self-esteem. Most of us have people in our lives who either have too much time on their hands and spend it interfering with our lives or don't feel good about themselves and do everything possible to bring us down to their level. Remember, your well-being and success are not contingent on the goodwill of others. As Anne suggests, don't even bother getting defensive—stay your course.

LESSONS LEARNED FROM TWENTY YEARS OF CONSULTING

I want to share with you my personal experiences with starting and leading my own business over the past twenty years. I've learned the hard way that when I talk about the things that have helped me succeed in my own business, I'm accused (often in the press) of being a braggart, self-absorbed, or self-important. There's a part of me that thinks if I were a man making the same claims, it would be construed as a modest manifesto of what it takes to be successful. But I'm not a man. So I decided to write about where I succeeded *and* where

I failed. Sometimes I think the failures were the best lessons, but the fact is that both were important to my development as an entrepreneurial leader. There were certain things that I did intuitively right. But make no mistake about it, there were certain things that I did intuitively wrong. I thought I had all the right instincts, but they didn't turn out the way I would have liked them to. The thumbs-up or thumbs-down sign below each lesson lets you know if I learned this by making a mistake or through good intuition.

If you've attended any of my presentations or read my previous books, you know that I began my career working in student affairs on college campuses. My greatest aspiration when I graduated from college was to be a residence hall director at a major university. I spent only a few years on that career track. The summer after I received my master's degree in counseling from a college where I was working as a dorm director, I was asked by the placement director if I would be interested in working for the summer for a company that needed someone to write job descriptions for them. I had nothing better to do and gladly accepted. I knew I was a pretty good writer, and I certainly could use the extra money—you don't become rich working on a college campus.

I reported for work with a subsidiary of the oil company ARCO (now BP) in the summer of 1976. I fully intended to stay only a few months and once the project was completed return to campus life. What I didn't know was that I would become intrigued with what was then called employee relations and with how much more money I could make. Each week I earned about what was equal to a month's pay in residential life. I dove into the assignment of writing job descriptions by interviewing people who were actually doing the job. In the process, I learned every job performed at the company and met many of the people who performed those jobs. When I completed the assignment in less than the time anticipated, I realized I would like to stay on with the company. So I wrote a proposal to the manager of human resources describing how I could assist him in meeting the challenges of hiring, recruiting, and motivating a diverse workforce. Fortunately for me, he had never had anyone make such a bold proposal and hired me on full time. Thus started what has been a three-decade career in human resources. I didn't know it at the time, but this was my first lesson in entrepreneurship and would change the course of my entire career.

ENTREPRENEURIAL LESSON 1
Market yourself.

After a relatively short time, I realized I was no more cut out to be a corporate employee than I was to work on an assembly line (which I actually did for about one week between semesters in college). The corporate structure, rules, and expectations were foreign to me. I quickly learned that reporting to work at 8:00 AM meant 8:00 AM, not 8:05 AM, and for ten years hated the routine. Then there was the whole hierarchy. Knowing your place was important to maintaining corporate egos—I never quite got that lesson. I thought organizations thrived on different opinions and thorough discussions of the issues. That may have been true in academia, but it certainly wasn't in the corporate world. I quickly learned to acquiesce to the opinions of the most senior people and to ask "How high?" when I was told to jump. I was lured into something I was not particularly well suited for by the promise of money and prestige.

ENTREPRENEURIAL LESSON 2
Never sell your soul to the devil.

When solicited to sign up for the company's 401(k) plan, I thought I couldn't possibly be with the company long enough to warrant joining up. In case you don't know, the 401(k) plan is a financial benefit: You contribute money to a retirement account, and the company matches your contribution. I was twenty-five years old and had my entire career ahead of me. Who needed a few extra bucks in an account I wouldn't be able to touch until I was fifty-five or sixty years old? In retrospect, *I did*. I missed out on "free money." All I had to do was contribute some small amount from every paycheck, and my money would've been doubled. But did I do that? Nooooooooo.

ENTREPRENEURIAL LESSON 3
Don't be shortsighted. Plan your financial future.

For the next five years, I worked in various positions in employee relations, which eventually became known as personnel and was later changed to human resources. The reason I kept transferring to new departments was because I became bored. *Been there. Done that. Give me something new to do* was my motto. Fortunately for me, the company had a tuition assistance program; in my fifth year, I started work on my doctorate, paid for largely by the company. Now *that* was something I did right. I got a forty-thousand-dollar education for about eight thousand. I still wasn't fulfilled and I was still living paycheck to paycheck, but I did get my doctorate in counseling psychology.

ENTREPRENEURIAL LESSON 4
When employed by a company, take advantage of the perks it offers that will help you to achieve your goals.

For as long as I could remember, I had a dream of becoming a psychologist. I wanted to help people, and I thought that this was the way to do it. But I never explored other alternatives. I never investigated whether that was a career for which I was suited. I didn't know any psychologists, and I didn't make an effort to speak with any to find out what a career in the field would mean in reality. Nevertheless, when I finally got my degree after five years of going to school at night and working full time in employee relations or human resources or whatever it was called at the time, I quit to open a private practice of psychotherapy. No one in my immediate network thought it was a good idea. My mother told me the thought of my being "unemployed" made her stomach churn. My best friend questioned why I would leave such a lucrative and prestigious position. After a relatively short time, I came to think that perhaps they were right. Sitting in a room all day—day after day—wasn't compatible with my energy level. I had traded one form of confinement for another.

ENTREPRENEURIAL LESSON 5
Know thyself.

So I decided I would offer public seminars for women in which I could help them become more assertive and make career decisions that would bring them to more empowered paths. I designed the program, bought mailing lists, contracted with hotels to hold the seminars, printed flyers, and . . . held my breath. Certainly women would want to attend one of my seminars, I thought. I had so much knowledge about women in the workplace. Well, you can probably guess what happened.

It was a struggle to break even on these programs. I asked friends to attend for free so that the paying attendees wouldn't feel they were part of a program for losers—or, worse yet, facilitated by a loser. I hadn't done enough research. I'd trusted my intuition too much. Public seminars are tough—it's why so many consultants focus on doing in-house programs, where you have a built-in clientele. Lesson learned. About this same time, my savings account was nearly empty. I had to take an equity line of credit against my home to make upcoming mortgage payments. In the twenty years that I have had my own business, I don't recall ever feeling such despair and questioning my ability to be successful on my own.

> **ENTREPRENEURIAL LESSON 6**
> Do your homework. Research and learn about best
> practices before diving in.

Then came a call that changed my life. It was from a woman I knew who managed the training department at a large corporation. She asked if I wanted to "coach" someone. You have to remember that in 1986, business coaches were not de rigueur. I didn't even know what it meant, but I did know I was willing to do whatever it took to get out of my professional doldrums. So I said, "Sure I can coach someone." Even though I had no clue where to start, I jumped in, putting together my knowledge of organizational and human behavior to develop one of the first models for business coaching. Of course, at the time I had no idea I was doing that; I knew only that I needed to pay my mortgage.

ENTREPRENEURIAL LESSON 7
Take risks consistent with your areas of expertise.

Before long I had a private practice of psychotherapy and a burgeoning coaching practice. I couldn't do both well. Whereas therapy required measured analysis, coaching required me to be bold and courageous in my observations. It felt like a tug-of-war going on inside me. I felt a commitment to the clients I had worked with for nearly two years, but my heart told me I was better suited for coaching. My greatest fear was that this move into the unknown would simply mean I was giving up yet another kind of stability. But I also knew I had to do something different for my own peace of mind.

And so I began speaking with my clients about my imminent departure from private practice, saying good-bye to them, and finding other therapists I thought could help them. No sooner did I do this than my phone started ringing with more coaching clients. Before I knew it, I had far more of these clients than I'd ever had therapy clients—and the compensation was exponentially more, because their companies were footing the bill.

ENTREPRENEURIAL LESSON 8
Trust that when one door closes, another will open.

For the next several years, I developed a corporate clientele consisting of some of the world's biggest and best companies. I traveled to Asia, to Europe, and throughout North America coaching people to achieve the broadest goals they were capable of—but had always missed because of messages learned in childhood about what it meant to be successful. I was working harder than ever, but loving every minute of it. The only problem was that I still wasn't earning what I needed to meet my definition of rich: *having all the money you need to live your life the way you want, free from concerns about money*. In some ways I was still being the nice girl I was taught to be in childhood—take care of others, be of service, work hard, and everything will be all right. But it wasn't. I was surviving in my own business, but not thriving.

One day, after a coaching session with a client I felt I wasn't prepared to help as much as he needed, I realized that one coach can't be expected to meet all of a client's needs. Corporations were paying good money for me to coach their employees, but I was limited by my own knowledge and expertise. I knew what I knew—and I knew what I didn't. Then it dawned on me that if each client could have a *team* of people to work with, he or she would have the best of all worlds. It also became evident that if I could put together a team of coaches under my umbrella, I would earn passive income from a percentage of their earnings.

ENTREPRENEURIAL LESSON 9
As a sole practitioner, you will find your earnings are limited by the number of hours in the day.

I called a meeting of colleagues who were starting their own coaching practices to discuss how we might work collaboratively. One of the women at the meeting I had known for several years and considered a good friend seemed to have a firm grasp on what I wanted to accomplish. After discussing it, although not at great length, we agreed we would start a company using a team-based coaching model—something no one else was doing at the time. She and I interviewed and formed a consortium of coaches, each an independent contractor, who would be part of a coaching team for each client. We would first do an assessment of the client's needs, then assemble coaches with expertise in the client's developmental areas.

She and I invested quite a bit of money and time in developing marketing materials and systems that formed the cornerstone of Corporate Coaching International. We shared a common vision of what we wanted to do, but not how we wanted to do it. She had a broader vision of where she wanted to take the business. I focused more narrowly on the quality of service we offered clients. On the surface, it should have been a match made in heaven—but it wasn't. We got the company rolling, but lost our friendship in the process. We both had successful individual practices, but weren't really prepared for what it meant to be business partners. After only two years, we divided the business in half and went our separate ways. It was an expensive and painful lesson.

ENTREPRENEURIAL LESSON 10
Choose your business partners carefully.

The biggest leap of faith I have had to make over the years has been believing that if I raised my fees, I wouldn't lose all my clients. When I was a sole practitioner, people were used to paying an hourly fee. As part of a team, I had to charge for the hourly fees of all the coaches *and* for my coordination of efforts and administrative costs. That's called *profit*. In other words, I would no longer earn money only for the work I performed; I would also earn money from the work *others* performed. But would my clients accept it? Quite frankly, some didn't. I lost a few along the way, but the increased fees more than made up for them. Now I was working smarter, not harder.

ENTREPRENEURIAL LESSON 11
Learn what you're worth, then charge what you're worth.

It was about this time that I decided I wanted to give something back to the community, so I started doing coaching and consulting with a few nonprofit agencies. Given the fact that the pockets of these organizations weren't as deep as corporate ones, I significantly reduced my fees to work with them. Word spread throughout the nonprofit community that I was affordable, and soon I personally was doing more work with nonprofits than for corporations. I no longer had time to service my corporate clients. What happened? My profit margin went down. This was another turning point for me. As much as I wanted to do good, I couldn't do well simultaneously. I had reverted to my "nice girl" persona.

After about a year of this, I finally realized that I had to establish some limits. I chose just a few causes that I really believed in and agreed to provide one day of service per month to them pro bono (at no charge) when they requested it. If a nonprofit called that was willing to pay the full fee, I would be happy to work with it. But if I reduced my fees for one community agency, I would have to do it for all of them or I would give the appearance of having an inconsistently applied fee schedule. Those who couldn't pay the full fee I referred to sole practitioners who needed the work and who could service the client well. As I said earlier, when one door closes, another opens. My corporate client list began to expand again.

ENTREPRENEURIAL LESSON 12
Vary your fee schedule judiciously.

Another fee lesson I learned the hard way cost me thousands of dollars over a period of time. I took a client to dinner around the holidays, we had a few drinks, and he started to negotiate fees with me. I told him I really didn't want to talk about money; I was taking him to dinner to thank him for the work he had given my firm over the year. But he persisted. To this day, I don't know if it was an intentional ploy to get me to reduce my fees, but I was in the holiday spirit, I'd had a few drinks, and I agreed to lower our consulting fee for his company.

He continued to be a good client, but my profit was diminished from that point forward. Each time our firm raised our fees, his were still lower than those of other clients. It's also not good business to reduce fees upon request. Again, if one client talks to another, it can create a lot of ill will. A better idea would have been to say I would be happy to reduce the fees if he would just let me know which services he would like to eliminate to make it more affordable for him.

ENTREPRENEURIAL LESSON 13
Don't talk money over drinks, at parties, or social events.

The business and my work-life balance grew in inverse proportions. The more successful I was, the less time I had to do the things I'd said I would when I'd left corporate America. I was doing everything myself and had no life. I recall the exact moment when I knew I had to hire someone to help me with the administrative detail. I was sitting in a client's office, and rather than listening to what she was saying I was thinking about all the administrivia I had to do that afternoon. I was breaking my own rule: *Be fully present in the moment.* Driving home that afternoon, I resolved to hire someone to help me.

That's the positive lesson here. The negative one is that I kept hiring all the wrong people. In the price range I wanted to pay, I wasn't getting the kind of quality person I needed to serve my clients well. My clients were big companies paying big bucks. The person who answered the phone and interacted with them had to be sharp, professional, and respectful. I became the Murphy Brown of assistants (you may recall the turnover outside her office door), and I wound up spending more time hiring and firing than the few extra dollars were worth.

Just about this time, I was in yet another client meeting that included a young woman working on her doctorate at a local college. I thought, *That's the kind of person I need.* Of course it would be unethical to offer a job to a client's employee, so I asked her if she knew of anyone like herself who might interested in a job. She did, and her friend came to work with me. I paid her nearly twice what I'd paid anyone else in the position, but I could also expand the role because she was smart and capable. If she did only enough to let me have a life again, I would be happy. To my surprise—she did all that and more.

With the right person working with me, I had more time to market, strategize, and better serve my clients. The year after she came on board, the business grew 50 percent. The next year, it grew another 50 percent. And it just keeps growing. That's the basis of the phrase *You pay in advance for capacity.* Some people call it spending money to make money. Business growth is dependent on investing in the things and people needed to be successful. If you're not willing to make the sacrifices needed to build a positive impression of your company or product, why do it at all?

Just as I wrote this last sentence, an e-mail popped up in my inbox from a client. Her last line was "Wanted to let you know that your staff is delightful to work with—prompt, friendly, helpful, efficient, everything you would ever want in a person representing you." How cool is that? Synchronicity at work!

ENTREPRENEURIAL LESSON 14
Don't do it alone. Find the right people to help you build your business and pay in advance for capacity.

As the business flourished, I began to relax. We had a group of core clients who used us on a regular basis. In fact, two or three really big corporations constituted about 80 percent of our business. I took the path of least resistance and stopped marketing. I started playing tennis again and went back to my photography. I guess you can say I rested on my laurels. Until September 11, that is. The entire game changed at that point, for a variety of reasons. The terrorist attacks wreaked havoc on small businesses as the economy went into a state of flux. Changes in senior management at our largest client, combined with economic concerns, caused the firm to reduce the use of our services by more than 90 percent. Our once plentiful flow of cash came to a grinding halt.

In December of that year (my sixteenth year in business), I began to wonder if my firm could survive. There were a few depressing weeks there when I wasn't quite sure what to do and how to turn the situation around. This was only compounded by my sharing the national mood of defeat following the attacks. By mid-January of the following year, though, I got my fighting spirit back. Nothing—not a terrorist attack or loss of clients—was going to stop me. I wasn't starting from scratch, but it sure felt like it.

ENTREPRENEURIAL LESSON 15
Never let down your guard. When the going gets good—keep doing those things that contributed to your success.

With the help of our staff and contractors, we got the business on its feet, but it took a few years to return to our previous profit margins. In the process, I lost some of my enthusiasm for running the business. I had just sold *Nice Girls Don't Get the Corner Office* to Warner Books and wanted to carve out time to market it when it was published. I also wanted to become a motivational speaker, but knew it was a very competitive business and, as such, had to be approached as just that—a business. So I started a parallel business, Drloisfrankel.com. My staff and I went to work learning about public speaking, attending workshops in the field (well, my staff did), and creating an infrastructure to support what I hoped would be an influx of new, different kinds of clients.

We worked for about a year putting this together before we got our first paid speaking gig. Little by little the calls came dribbling in. There was no way I could earn a living at this rate, but it was a start. Once *Nice Girls Don't Get the Corner Office* hit the bookstores and the promotion began, it was a different game. The calls were now pouring in, and my vision of becoming a motivational speaker came true. As the cliché goes, though, be careful what you wish for. We were suddenly juggling the coaching business and the speaking business. Time for more staff—in this case, someone to take my place managing the coaching business. Had we not built a solid foundation, I don't think we could have handled the influx of inquiries and engagements. Yet another example of *you pay in advance for capacity.*

ENTREPRENEURIAL LESSON 16

Have a clear vision of what you want to do and work to create the systems needed to support it in anticipation of success.

I was flush with excitement about the possibilities. Whereas the coaching business had previously focused on corporate clients, we were now getting calls from individuals who had read the book and wanted coaching. I could envision us offering a new line of coaching services geared to individual clients who would be paying out of their own pockets. It required a new fee structure to be able meet budgets more modest than those on a corporate scale. It also required bigger office space. For years we'd kept our overhead to a minimum through relatively small offices. We didn't need more space—we usually went to our corporate clients' offices. But now individual clients would be coming to us.

At about the same time, the office suite next to ours became available. It was perfect to create a conference room, guest coach office, and an additional waiting area, so we rented that suite, too—doubling the cost of office rent. It'll be okay, I thought. *Pay in advance for capacity.* But I relied too much on my intuition and didn't do enough research. Yes, the individual clients were calling, but most couldn't afford our services even at a reduced rate. We paid our coaches two hundred dollars an hour, and most coaching sessions were ninety minutes to two hours. And that was for just one session. We knew good coaching would take four to six sessions and that we had to pay for overhead as well as make a profit. We designed a coaching program for these individual clients that would cost about $2,200—a fraction of what our corporate clients paid for more robust coaching programs.

You may be thinking about now that *you* wouldn't make a $2,200 investment in your career. Well, neither would anyone else. We shifted to charging an hourly fee for services performed, but even at that, we weren't covering our expenses. After eighteen months, we decided it wasn't such a good idea after all, changed direction, went back to working with primarily corporate clients, and moved back into a smaller office space. In short, my intuition and vision weren't enough. I hadn't learned my lesson from the public seminars fiasco. I should have done more research.

> ## ENTREPRENEURIAL LESSON 17
> **Do your homework. Research and learn about best practices before diving in. (I had to learn this lesson twice.)**

Now, as I enter into my twentieth year leading my own business, I've learned many lessons and no doubt have yet to learn more. As you can see by counting the thumbs up and down, I've learned more from my mistakes than I have from successes. I've achieved my financial goals, helped a lot of people along the way, and maintained my integrity and values in the process. I've learned that I'm tougher than I thought I was. I've put beans on my own table—and the tables of those who work with me—for all these years. My worst day leading my own business is still better than my best day working for someone else. If I did it—*you can, too.*

Coaching Tips for Women Entrepreneurs

73. **Follow Mrs. Fields's recipe for success.** Debbi Fields, founder of Mrs. Fields Cookies, once said it was all about *passion, persistence, and perfection.* Whether it's starting a non-profit organization or a for-profit business, you're going to put a lot of time and energy into it. Your focus has to be directed toward something you are so passionate about doing—and doing well—that nothing can deter you from success.

74. **Think and act big.** When Tom Watson founded IBM (International Business Machine Corporation), he had no international business, but he envisioned that one day he would. When Jamie Foxx accepted the Academy Award for the starring role in the movie *Ray,* he thanked his grandmother for teaching him to "act like you've been somewhere." Big is relative. You may never aspire, for example, to be the biggest animal rescue agency, but you should act as if you already are. Doing so causes you to see things and consider options you would otherwise overlook or think impossible. When I started my business, I put thousands of dollars into marketing materials at a time when I could ill afford to do so. But it made me look and feel competitive. I had to live up to the "big" image I conveyed to potential clients—and eventually my firm became it.

75. **Be a servant-leader.** Contrary to popular belief, entrepreneurial leadership isn't about *you*—it's about others. It's about your clients, customers, constituents, followers, and the communities in which you operate. In 1970, Robert Greenleaf coined the term *servant-leadership* to describe how vision combined with a

service ethic contributes to not only leadership success but the quality of society as well. The highest priority of the servant-leader is to ensure that the needs of others are met first—which is what makes *women* such natural servant-leaders.

76. **Learn the language of money.** In my book *Nice Girls Don't Get Rich: 75 Avoidable Mistakes Women Make with Money,* I talked about the fact that women are less likely to understand the basics of money and investing than men. Regardless of the size or nature of your venture, you need to understand how to make it profitable. Even the term *nonprofit* is misleading. These institutions can't operate at a loss and remain successful. As an entrepreneurial leader, you'll be involved with budgeting, investing, payrolls, or other forms of money management. Take a course in finance for non-financial managers at your local community college; start reading *The Wall Street Journal* and other money magazines.

77. **Expect and prepare for setbacks.** When you're running your own show, there are inevitable bumps in the road. By anticipating them, you're more likely to view them as challenges to be overcome than insurmountable obstacles that cause you to fail. Developing a network of similarly minded friends and colleagues who can encourage you and help you over the hurdles is critical for entrepreneurs.

78. **Keep an "atta gal" file.** There are days in the lives of all entrepreneurs when we wonder what the heck we're doing and why we're doing it. We may hear praise from ten clients or customers, then get one piece of negative feedback that makes us question our direction and decision to lead our own enterprise. Keep a file of notes from satisfied people, press clip-

pings, or other indications that you've done well and pull it out on those days you need a little encouragement.

79. **Be a continual learner.** Too often, entrepreneurs become so involved in day-to-day operations and challenges that they miss new trends or information that could help them to remain competitive. Couple that with the fact that women often have additional family responsibilities, and it seems as if there's never enough time to stay current. Each week, schedule a thirty-minute meeting with yourself where you read a professional journal or in other ways spend time staying up to date in your field. It's the only way to grow professionally along with those you serve.

80. **Network, network, network.** Not only will your networks help bring attention to your product or service, but they'll also provide you with the connections that you need to run your business efficiently and a stream of information to keep you current in your industry.

81. **Choose a hospitable location.** If you're going to open a swimming pool store, Anchorage may not be the place to bring you maximum success. Similarly, if you provide a service that's geared toward a particular industry, you want to be geographically close to the headquarters of such companies. Check out the Web site http://epodunk.com for valuable information related to household income, education level, average age, and more for a particular city.

82. **Ask for help.** One of the biggest mistakes a business owner can make is thinking she has to go it alone. There's no need for you to reinvent the wheel when there are people out there who have been there, done that. Many cities have free services

for small-business owners, and there are business coaches who cater to entrepreneurs.

83. ***Consider affiliated entrepreneurships or franchises.*** If you want to be self-employed but don't have a particular service or product you want to sell, the support offered by affiliations and franchises may be the way to go. Attend a franchise expo (you can find them online) where you can find out more about opportunities at various levels of investment.

84. ***Explore bartering.*** Many business owners, myself included, simultaneously save money and build their networks by exchanging goods and services without exchanging money. For example, maybe you own a printing company, while I need new letterhead and business cards. You mention to me that you're having a problem with a particular employee, and I suggest that coaching might be effective. In a barter arrangement, I would provide coaching and you would provide me with the printed items I need. This can be a little tricky, because both parties have to feel as if they're getting a fair deal in the process—otherwise relationships and reputations can be damaged. That's why you want to be clear up front about the cost or value of the items being bartered.

85. ***Check out SCORE.*** The SCORE Association (Service Corps of Retired Executives) is a nonprofit association dedicated to entrepreneur education and the formation, growth, and success of small businesses nationwide. Its purpose is to strengthen the US small-business community through experienced volunteer members who provide high-quality technical and managerial counseling and guidance to prospective and existing small-business owners and nonprofit organizations. SCORE members advise their clients to take a balanced ap-

proach to management and to enhance the potential for the success of their business through quality education and counseling on specific problems in areas such as finance, personnel, marketing, production, and merchandising. They also urge clients, when appropriate, to seek sound advice and useful relationships with other professional business specialists and associates. There are SCORE programs in various cities throughout the United States; you will often find them affiliated with your local SBA (Small Business Administration).

86. *Read* **Leading at the Speed of Growth: Journey from Entrepreneur to CEO** by Katherine Catlin and Jana Matthews. Using anecdotes from successful entrepreneurs, this book helps you understand the phases that growing companies go through and the different roles you must play in each phase.

CHAPTER NINE

Raising Our Daughters to Lead

One is not born a woman, one becomes one.
—Simone de Beauvoir

One of the questions I am consistently asked by the men and women I meet as I travel around the world is: *What can I do to raise a self-confident daughter?* Even girls who grow up in homes where they are encouraged to be and do whatever they choose find that once they go out into the world, they are bombarded with social messages about how they should look or behave. It starts in childhood and lasts long into adulthood. One woman from Denver told me that she dresses her preschool daughter in a way that allows for maximum mobility. The child came home one day and told her that her teacher suggested she dress more like a "girl." A woman from Chicago told me that she intentionally sent her daughter to an all-girl high school so that she would learn to express herself freely and develop a healthy sense of herself as a woman. When the school competes in academic contests, the girls from coed schools taunt them with shouts of "Where are the guys?" Schools, television, music, and advertising continue to emphasize the feminine ideal.

At best, young girls are getting the right message at home but still receive conflicting social messages. The American Association of University Women (AAUW) has conducted extensive research on how young women and men are treated differently throughout their academic experiences. Here are some of the findings cited in the group's report *How Schools Shortchange Girls:*

- Girls receive significantly less attention from classroom teachers than boys.

- African American girls have fewer interactions with teachers than do white girls, despite evidence that they attempt to initiate interactions more frequently.

- Sexual harassment of girls by boys—from innuendo to actual assault—in our nation's schools is increasing.

- The contributions and experiences of girls and women are still marginalized or ignored in many textbooks.

- Differences between girls and boys in math achievement are small and declining. Yet in high school, girls are still less likely than boys to take the most advanced courses and be in the top-scoring math groups.

- The gender gap in science is not decreasing and may be increasing.

- Even girls who are competent in math and science are much less likely to pursue scientific or technological careers than are their male classmates.

- There is a drop in girls' math confidence followed by a drop in math achievement in the middle-school years.

Numerous studies reveal that the self-confidence and lack of self-consciousness exhibited by pre-adolescent girls diminishes once they reach adolescence. One study conducted by Elaine Bell Kaplan asked culturally and racially diverse college students to recount childhood experiences. It's interesting to note that most of the women in the study remembered being "self-assured and assertive" between the ages of nine and ten. *All* of the women remembered this as a time when their relationships with their best friends were "much more important to their sense of self and their ability to develop nurturing relationships than were relations with boys."

Once they reached adolescence, however, things changed. By the age of eleven, physical appearances and acting in ways considered appropriate for girls became more of a focus from family and friends alike. If they were overweight, they were chided by boys and cautioned by well-meaning parents. If they acted a bit too tomboyish, they learned that their sexual preference would come into question. From this point on, much of their self-worth was determined by body image. "It's a process of feminization as their identity becomes tied to feminine expressions while they are learning to conform to the norms and rules governing femininity," says Kaplan.

Clearly, there's work still to be done by all of us if we are to help young women who aspire to leadership roles to succeed in these endeavors—and encourage those who may never have thought about it to explore opportunities to lead. Conforming to the norms and rules of society shouldn't mean sublimating one's best self just to fit in.

BEST PARENTING PRACTICES

If you want to provide your daughter with the best chances for success later in life, start by doing all those things necessary to contribute to high self-esteem and self-confidence. That's not to say *all* children have the temperament or desire to eventually become leaders, or that you can never become a leader if your parents didn't nurture self-confidence. But I am saying that focusing on how you parent can give your daughter a leg up later in life—regardless of what she chooses to do.

Some of the earliest battles between you and your daughter will revolve around how she wants to dress. So many mothers lose sight of how they can use a daughter's choice of clothing to foster independence and freedom of expression. Dr. Pam Brill, an author, psychologist, and the mother of four talented, self-confident daughters, told me that she learned this lesson very early and with her first daughter:

> *From the time she was very young, my first daughter delighted in choosing the clothes she wore to day care. She would leave the house looking like it was Halloween or as if Jackson Pollock painted her. She even went through a period of intentionally wearing mismatched socks—which in some way made her feel secure. Other parents would look at her and wonder why she couldn't match her clothes or why I didn't care enough to dress her in a color-coordinated manner or to dress her at all. I just had to ignore it. As a working mom, I knew I could get very weary trying to fight every battle or worrying about what other parents thought about my mothering. I consciously chose to focus exerting my parental authority on primarily safety and health issues.*

Pam was smart enough to know that life with children is filled with conflicts much more important than what they wear—but not all parents are secure enough to think this way. Many parents, especially narcissistic ones, feel a child's dress is a reflection on the parent and insist that it be a *positive* reflection. This is more damaging than may be apparent on the surface. Psychologist Alan Rappoport, in his article "Co-Narcissism: How We Accommodate to Narcissistic Parents," claims that wanting your child to act in *your* best interest instead of your acting in hers can result in three things:

- The child accepting your values and behaviors as her own and not forging independent thinking.
- The child becoming compliant and acting in extreme ways to please you.
- Rebellion or acting in oppositional ways just to maintain a sense of self.

You'll notice that nowhere on the list does it say the result will be self-confidence and high self-esteem. If you want your daughters to have the capacity to lead later in life—whether that's leading a family, a team, a business, or a country—then you must recognize and reinforce your daughter's choices from an early age. That includes the choice of dress, friends, hairstyle, preferred room decor, and toys, among other things. There will of course be times when safety or the need to teach appropriate social skills precludes this from happening, but the decision to intervene should be made carefully and consciously. The general parenting philosophy *Because I'm the mommy and I said so* doesn't cut it.

Honor Your Daughter's Unique Gifts

It's one thing to allow your daughter to make her own choices. It's another to support and honor her unique preferences and proclivities. Whereas the former is about what she does, the latter is about who she is. We all know parents who push children in particular directions with the best of intentions but the worst of outcomes. That's because they don't understand their child's *inherent* personality traits. Instead, they ask the child to behave in ways that they themselves might, but that are incompatible with her nature. She may go along with it, and perhaps even excel in areas the parent prefers, but it doesn't mean this will bring out the best in your daughter.

Let me give you an example here using my own mother and how she parented me, her only daughter. My mother was outgoing, charming, and good at building relationships with just about anyone—even strangers she sat next to on the airplane. When I was a child, she would put me in social situations where I was encouraged to interact with others in much the same way she would. I cannot tell you how painful it was. By nature, I'm shy and introspective (which is why I can spend so many hours alone writing books!), although you would never know that upon meeting me. For years I pushed myself into social situations and careers that met my mother's expectations, but that never really allowed me to excel, which in turn caused me to think there *must* be something wrong with me. I don't think it's a coincidence that it wasn't until after she passed away that I reached my professional and personal stride. Without judgment or criticism (implied or otherwise), I was able to gravitate toward doing the things I most love—and did them far better than the things I thought I *should* be doing.

I wish the book *Nurture by Nature* had been around all those years ago. It's based on the Myers-Briggs Type Indicator (MBTI), and if you've read any of my past books you know that's the one standardized personality inventory I believe in and recommend that people learn more about. In a nutshell, the MBTI measures personality preferences, which are like filters through which we experience the world. These preferences are actually formed by the time we're four years old, give or take a year or two. They shape everything from the career we ultimately choose to the partner we choose to spend our lives with. *Nurture by Nature* authors Paul D. Tieger and Barbara Barron-Tieger do a wonderful job of explaining type and how it can be useful in parenting. I had the opportunity to ask Paul Tieger about the importance of nurturing a child by her nature:

> *Self-esteem and confidence come from being recognized and valued for who you are. Most parents don't understand who their kids are and instead expect them to be like themselves or their other children. This can lead to invalidating who a child really is. As a result, a child can spend her entire life trying to get that validation from others. Confidence comes from using your strengths. Women and girls who are "thinking types" are often not validated for it. It's one reason why women like Hillary Clinton or Martha Stewart have a tough time of it. The healthiest way for parents to encourage girls to achieve their full potential is to recognize and validate their preferences.*

Along these same lines, avoid the inclination to expect the same behaviors or talents from each child. Maybe you're not the narcissistic parent who expects your children to behave like you, but do you fall into the trap of expecting them to behave like one another? Has the phrase *Why can't you be more like your brother?* ever crossed your lips? Or how about *If your sister can get straight A's, so can you*? Honoring your children's gifts doesn't mean you make them do what *you* want them to do. It means you recognize the unique talents and preferences of each one of them as individuals. Dr. Brill provides a few more best-parenting suggestions for how to do this:

- Really *listen* to your daughter. Giving her your undivided attention when she talks to you makes her feel as if her voice is important and worthy of being heard.

- Follow your child's lead without judgment. Take care not to use veiled or implied judgment statements such as *Wouldn't you really rather . . .* or *Don't you think that it would be better if . . .* Even a child knows this means *you* would rather or *you* think it would be better.

- Model the messages that you want your daughter to internalize. If you want her to be goal-oriented, then set your own goals, talk about them, and let her see you working toward them. Success isn't inherited; it's passed down.

Instill a Competitive Spirit

When it comes to being competitive, women have traditionally been at a disadvantage. Not only have many young girls been excluded from childhood activities that instill healthy competition, but when they do act competitive, they risk being derided in any of a number of ways. As a result, they are reluctant to compete at full tilt (if at all), and they sidestep opportunities to lead. Parents can turn this around by providing experiential opportunities that instill a competitive spirit. Dr. Tammy Wong, you may recall from a previous chapter, is chief strategy officer for the partner organization of Sun Microsystems. One of the best-parenting practices she shared with me that no one else did was that she and her husband intentionally chose a gender-neutral name for her daughter— Jordan Taylor Wong. It was a name that people wouldn't assume belonged to a man or a woman when they looked at her résumé. "I thought Jordan Taylor Wong would be a good name for a CEO if that's what she wanted to become," says Wong. And like many parents, to instill a competitive spirit and sense of adventure Tammy has gotten Jordan involved in both individual and team sports since the age of six. It's not important to Tammy that Jordan becomes a world-class athlete. She's not even concerned if her daughter fails at the sports in which she participates. What is important to her is that Jordan not be afraid of trying new things.

This notion of enrolling your daughter in both individual *and* team sports is critical. Several of the women I spoke with pointed out that the skills learned in each arena are uniquely important. Whereas an individual sport encourages your daughter to achieve her *personal* best, a team sport teaches her the fundamentals of being a member of a group that depends on her participation. Watching the Olympics or other sporting events, you can see the differences in the athletes who are individual versus team participants. Whereas the gymnasts are insularly focused on their own performances, the members of the volleyball, hockey, basketball, or softball teams share a sense of camaraderie and awareness of others that's equally important to success.

When I asked Barbara Stanny, author of *Prince Charming Isn't Coming, Secrets of Six-Figure Women,* and *Overcoming Undearning,* how she managed to raise three high-achieving, self-confident daughters, she decided to ask them. Each one of them that said a defining influence in her life was Barbara's insistence that she do what she feared most because that's what would enable her to grow. Daughter Melissa, now thirty-three, told her mom, "You'd always say it's okay to be afraid, but to never, ever let that fear stop you from taking risks, or from taking the next step to where you want to go."

Another consideration in helping daughters develop a competitive spirit is the decision to have them attend single-sex schools. I recently had the opportunity to address the young women of Immaculate Heart High School in Los Angeles. Like many all-girl schools, its mission is to provide educational opportunities that foster self-esteem and achieving one's full potential. I was impressed with the confidence and self-assurance these students exhibited. During the question-and-answer portion of my presentation, they were not hesitant to speak up (which is more than I can say for some of the corporate women I work with) and asked insightful questions about the realities of women in the workplace. The question then becomes: What are the pros and cons of sending your daughter to an all-girl school?

One study of more than 4,200 women who graduated from all-girl schools, conducted in 2000 by Goodman Research Group, found that:

- 93 percent agreed that girls' schools provide greater leadership opportunities.
- 91 percent felt girls' schools are more relevant to young women's academic needs.
- 87 percent felt young women should be encouraged to attend girls' schools.

RAISING OUR DAUGHTERS TO LEAD   255

- 85 percent felt girls' schools provide young women with more encouragement in the areas of science, math, and technology than coed schools.
- 72 percent felt girls' schools are more relevant to young women's personal and social needs.
- 71 percent felt more prepared to transition to college than their counterparts from coed schools.
- 85 percent felt themselves better prepared academically than their counterparts.
- 63 percent felt girls' schools prepare young women for the "real world."
- Girls' school graduates consistently outscored females and males nationwide on both sections of the SAT, with scores on average as much as 20 percent higher.
- 94 percent of respondents had attended or were attending college.
- 80 percent of respondents held leadership positions since graduating.

If single-sex education yields such positive results for girls, why don't more parents choose to give their daughters the competitive advantage by sending them to all-girl schools? The arguments include that it doesn't represent the real world and therefore limits the opportunity to learn important coping and social skills; that it removes opportunities for discussion that could eventually change the nature of coed education; that it's elitist and expensive; that public schools are better-funded and therefore provide better equipment, teachers, and curricula; and that removing girls from coed schools contributes to boys' underachievement.

The advantages and disadvantages of sending any child to a

single-sex school are something that families must weigh vis-à-vis their individual values, philosophy, and financial situation. Not only does the decision impact your daughter, but it can also impact her male siblings, existing friendships and social networks, and a family's natural rhythm (having to take children to different schools, attend different events, and the like). Nonetheless, if you want to increase a girl's chances of success, her self-confidence, and the likelihood that she will be prepared to lead, it's clear that providing a single-sex education might be the key.

Encourage Financial Independence

In my book *Nice Girls Don't Get Rich: 75 Avoidable Mistakes Women Make with Money,* I talk about the complex relationship women have with money:

> *Despite the fact that in childhood most of us get all the right messages about the importance of being financially independent, we do all the wrong things when it comes to accumulating the amount of wealth we need to be truly financially independent. Why? Because throughout our lives we're given multiple, often conflicting messages. On the one hand, we're taught about the value of money and the need to spend and save it wisely. On the other, we're implicitly or explicitly taught that it's equally important to be kind, nurturing, and collaborative; that our real roles revolve less around money and more around relationships.*
>
> *This double bind causes little girls to limit their interest in acquiring wealth and ultimately their capacity to acquire it. They don't aspire to get rich, they can't see themselves as rich, or they reduce their opportunities to get rich. . . .*

Speaking with women around the world about getting rich, I got the distinct feeling they were uncomfortable talking about money. It was as if the word rich *was a four-letter word. Whereas a woman may be called a "rich bitch," there are no similarly pejorative terms to describe a man. And Lord knows we avoid the b-word even more than we avoid talking about money! It doesn't seem to matter if you're twenty-five or fifty-five. As a woman you are less likely to focus on methods for becoming rich and more likely to focus on "doing good."*

"Nice girls" don't get rich in large part because of the social messages they receive when they are growing up:

- *Money is power, and most little girls are not taught to be powerful—they're taught to be "nice."*
- *Girls are socialized to be caretakers, nurturers, and accommodators in society—not necessarily breadwinners.*
- *As child bearers and caretakers women often work discontinuously and are penalized for it. Alternatively they're put on something demeaningly referred to as the "mommy track."*
- *Women are more likely to spend their income on their children and the household, whereas men are more likely to be prudent about investing.*
- *Women are reluctant to ask for wages, perks, or raises reflective of the value they add to their organizations because they're not sure they "deserve" it.*

Financial literacy and independence contribute not only to self-esteem and self-confidence but to freedom of choice as well. Unless your wealth is inherited, acquiring it also requires a degree of competitiveness. Being free to choose includes the ability to start your own business, leave a low-paying job or one where you're being treated poorly, or move into a leadership role. Like it or not, money is power. Until women pay more attention to getting their fair share of the world's wealth, they will remain dependent on men and miss opportunities to play leading roles. That's why best-parenting practices include teaching your daughters about money. There are a number of ways you can do this. Author and executive coach Dr. Karen Otazo reports on one technique that worked when she was raising her own daughter:

> Teach your daughter about fiscal responsibility in her early teens by giving her an allowance that's put into a bank account with enough money for reasonable purchases and expenses so she can pay her own bills. She should be in charge of this account with you having oversight. By the time she's in her midteens, she can be given a credit card with a spending limit and responsibility for paying it in full each month. Similarly, any money received through gifts or inheritance should be divided into savings, spending, and charity.

A few other suggestions for raising financially astute (and hopefully, rich) daughters include:

- In restaurants, give your daughter money to pay the bill and ask that she make sure she's received the correct change.
- In addition to a base allowance, provide money for completing specified chores in a *timely and acceptable* manner.
- Teach your daughter how to read a savings account or other investment statement.

- Play Monopoly together.
- When discussing careers, include a conversation about associated incomes and how they impact life choices.
- Help your daughter develop a budget and stick with it by not supplementing funds once her money has been spent or put into savings.
- Use money to help very young girls learn how to count.
- Show your daughter how to comparison-shop.
- Charge interest on "loans" so your daughter can learn how interest accumulates.
- Visit http://childrensfinancialnetwork.com.

Outside the Home

As I said earlier, you can be doing all the right things at home only to find that attitudes and behaviors in the community have an impact on your daughter's self-esteem and confidence. The "mean-girls" phenomenon is unfortunately something very real that parents must stay attuned to and take seriously. Technology has made it easier for both boys and girls to harass their peers in anonymous and unhealthy ways. Nasty e-mails, text messages, and blogs are all too often targeted at young women as opposed to young men. Dr. Brill offers these suggestions to parents:

- Monitor what's coming in and going out from your daughter's computer or handheld devices to be certain she isn't being victimized or victimizing others with malicious messages. Engage her in this so it doesn't look like you're spying. Let her know that you trust her—it's the other people out there that concern you.

- Watch for changes in friends, grades, social interactions, and communication with you. Lower grades in school, less communication with you, or frequent changes in friends can all be signs that she's struggling with peer relationships. Maintain an ongoing dialogue about these things so it doesn't surprise her when you talk about the shifts.

- Get involved with the school and build relationships with your daughter's teachers. Communicate your expectation that the school will have a zero-tolerance policy for harassment and ask teachers to notify you if they see any changes in your daughter's behavior, mood, or academic achievements. Be sure to let her and the school know that you want to be informed if your own daughter is playing a part in excluding or scapegoating other girls, too.

- Accountability goes both ways. Talk candidly with your daughter about the mean-girls phenomenon, including the subtle behaviors and attitudes that it includes. Offer your observations and insights when you think she might be getting caught up in this type of thing. Suggest ways to avoid such behaviors, and give her support when she tells you just how hard that is in today's school and social settings. Also, be aware that not all parents hold to this accountability principle; many will go to the mat to defend their own kids' bullying behaviors.

- If necessary, don't hesitate to get professional help for your daughter at the first sign of emotional turmoil. Don't wait for it to get so bad that she becomes clinically depressed or loses a significant degree of self-confidence.

AAUW RECOMMENDATIONS FOR SCHOOLS, PARENTS, AND STUDENTS

The American Association of University Women does a wonderful job of researching trends related to women and girls in education. One particular publication, *Growing Smart: What's Working for Girls in School* (executive summary and action guide), is filled with great ideas for how we can all ensure that young women get the education and experiences needed to make a difference by going out into the world with self-confidence. Here are just a few of the suggestions to parents contained in that document:

- Participate in frameworks such as the PTA to create change in schools. Initiate discussions about gender equity and ask teachers and administrators to implement some of the ideas described above.

- Require the same effort and achievement from sons and daughters. Encourage girls and boys to pursue math and science, and to consider nontraditional careers.

- Support your daughter's athletic achievements. Sponsor the teams, attend the games, and ensure that girls' teams are equitably funded.

- Recognize that high-achieving girls may be torn between academic and social success. Form support groups for girls and their families who face similar problems.

Also, make sure schools and teachers follow these AAUW recommendations:

- Ask teachers and students to identify needs not being met by current programming.

- Build ties with community groups such as Big Brothers Big Sisters, Girl Scouts, and Boys and Girls Clubs.

- Consider short-term experimentation with single-sex classes to boost girls' lagging math and science skills or to prepare girls for better mixed-group interaction.

- Teach conflict-resolution skills and adopt a clear school policy and grievance procedure on sexual harassment.

- Create an atmosphere in which girls feel comfortable aspiring, achieving, and excelling. Communicate high expectations for girls.

- Solicit help from parents, youth groups, and community leaders in implementing ideas that promote girls' achievement.

- Encourage girls to excel in math and science. Bring girls into classroom discussions and make learning about these subjects fun and relevant to them.

- Adopt gender-equitable teaching strategies. Require the same effort from girls and boys; pay as much attention to compliant students as to disruptive ones; create both mixed- and single-sex discussion groups.

- Expose girls to nontraditional careers. Invite women and men from nontraditional professions to visit the classroom and take field trips to high-tech companies.

- Select textbooks and reading materials free of sexual and racial stereotyping.

A FEW MORE SUGGESTIONS FROM COOL MOMS

So many women provided me with suggestions for how to prepare our daughters to lead that I can't possibly include or expand on each one. Instead, I'll thank Amy Reichbach, mother of two daughters a generation apart in age; Terry Monahan, mother of a Northeastern University senior; Mary Ann Chory, mother of a high school junior; and Carol Frohlinger, mother of an adult daughter, for the following tips:

- Always answer your daughter's questions honestly without dumbing down.
- If there is a problem in school, encourage your daughter to solve it on her own first; step in to help only if requested.
- Read her *Ms. Magazine*'s *Stories for Free Children*.
- When exploring "What do you want to be when you grow up?" include non-gender-traditional jobs as well, as if it's perfectly natural that a girl might want to be an entomologist, construction worker, or architect.
- Take your daughter to work and let her see what you do and how you do it.
- Keep your maiden name.
- Be mindful about how you raise your sons, teaching them about equality and expecting them to treat girls and women respectfully.
- Choose female pediatricians, lawyers, accountants, et cetera, so that your daughters have role models in significant occupations.
- Teach your daughter to do her "job" well. While she's in school, that means studying, participating as a family member, and being a productive member of the community.

Coaching Tips for Raising Our Daughters to Lead

87. **Validate who your daughter is, not who you want her to be.** Read the book *Nurture by Nature* to learn more about personality styles and how you can instill self-confidence and self-esteem by honoring your child's unique gifts and preferences.

88. **Encourage participation in individual and team sports.** Your daughter may never become an Olympic athlete, but learning how to compete, be a team member, and deal with wins and losses are valuable lessons that will serve her well throughout her lifetime.

89. **Foster independent thinking and decision making.** Allow your daughter to choose her own clothing, order from a menu, and have her own opinions—all of which may differ from your choices.

90. **Consider an all-girl school.** Studies show that girls who attend a single-sex school are more apt to develop skill in leadership and are more likely to excel in math and science, gravitate toward nontraditional careers, and have more self-esteem than girls who attend coed schools. Some states are even piloting programs for girls in the public schools. Find out if your district is one of them, and if it's not, learn about how these programs might be implemented.

91. **Enroll your daughter in a self-defense class.** Not only do these programs teach girls how to physically protect themselves, but they instill a sense of self-confidence that extends to other areas of her life as well.

92. **Teach your daughter about money.** From an early age, provide her with a bank account, an allowance, and guidelines for how to earn, save, and spend money.

93. **Get involved with your daughter's school.** Communicate

your expectations for how girls will be treated and taught. Insist that the school develop and enforce zero tolerance for harassment.

94. **Identify extracurricular activities suited to your daughter's personality.** Not all girls may want to join Brownies, Girl Scouts, or Campfire Girls, but it's important that she participate in programs that allow her to develop her leadership skills or find her unique voice. An acting, writing, or art class can also achieve these ends.

95. **Raise your sons to respect women.** Boys who learn from an early age that girls are different but equal are more likely to grow up to be men who will encourage rather than be threatened by powerful women. Convey overt messages about equality between the sexes and discourage boys from engaging in behavior that in any way puts down or minimizes girls and women.

96. **Teach your daughter skills for recognizing and responding to inappropriate social messages.** Talk to her about the ways in which she may encounter unwanted sexual advances, harassment, or other forms of sexism and help her to develop the language needed to address it when she encounters it.

97. **Model the way.** Your daughter will learn about leadership and self-confidence from watching you. Make sure you have developed your own communication, assertiveness, social, and leadership skills so that she can see what they look like in real time.

98. **Focus on your daughter's emotional intelligence.** She may be smart and self-confident, but does your daughter get along with other kids? Can she regulate her emotions? Is she empathetic? Too many parents breathe a sigh of relief when

they realize they have an exceptionally talented daughter and fail to ensure she also has the social skills that accompany success.

99. ***Expose your daughter to nontraditional activities and careers.*** If you can't afford to take her to Washington, DC, to learn how our government works, then sit down with her at the computer and explore international women politicians. If you're at a restaurant that is owned by a woman, ask to introduce her to the owner. Seize every opportunity to let her know there's a big world waiting for her, and she's limited only by her choices.

Reading List

There are so many books, articles, and periodicals on leadership that it would be impossible to include them all. Exclusion from this list isn't a reflection on the quality or value of a book—I simply want to make suggestions based on the material I've read, liked, and found helpful in shaping my own thinking about leadership and its component parts. Some books profess to know *the* secrets of leadership, but my own belief is that (1) you must be a leader for your time, which means giving your followers what *they* need, not what *you* want; (2) as with the women in this book, your leadership style will emerge based on your own experiences; and (3) it's important to be a perpetual student of leadership. It's not important *which* leadership books you read, it's important *that* you read. Doing so will contribute to your knowledge base in this broad discipline we call *leadership*.

Books

Urgent Message from Mother: Gather the Women, Save the World. Jean Shinoda Bolen, MD (Conari Press, 2005).

The Emotional Intelligence Quick Book: Everything You Need to

Know to Put Your EQ to Work. Dr. Travis Bradberry and Dr. Jean Greaves (Fireside, 2005).

The Disease to Please: Curing the People-Pleasing Syndrome. Harriet Braiker (McGraw-Hill, 2002).

Hit the Ground Running: A Woman's Guide to Success for the First 100 Days on the Job. Liz Cornish (McGraw-Hill, 2006).

Enlightened Power: How Women Are Transforming the Practice of Leadership. Lin Coughlin, Ellen Wingard, and Keith Hollihan (Jossey-Bass, 2005).

Nice Girls Don't Get the Corner Office: 101 Unconscious Mistakes Women Make That Sabotage Their Careers. Lois P. Frankel, PhD (Warner Books, 2004).

The Girl's Guide to Starting Your Own Business: Candid Advice, Frank Talk, and True Stories for the Successful Entrepreneur. Caitlin Friedman and Kimberly Yorio (Collins, 2005).

Leadership the Eleanor Roosevelt Way: Timeless Strategies from the First Lady of Courage. Robin Gerber (Portfolio, 2002).

Servant Leadership: A Journey into the Nature of Legitimate Power and Greatness. Robert Greenleaf (Paulist Press, 2002).

The Tao of Leadership: Lao Tzu's Tao Te Ching Adapted for a New Age. John Heider (Humanics Publishing Group, 1986).

Her Place at the Table: A Woman's Guide to Negotiating Five Key Challenges to Leadership Success. Deborah Kolb, Judith Williams, and Carol Frohlinger (Jossey-Bass, 2004).

The Shadow Negotiation: How Women Can Master the Hidden Agendas That Determine Bargaining Success. Deborah Kolb and Judith Williams (Simon & Schuster, 2000).

A Force for Change: How Leadership Differs from Management. John Kotter, PhD (Free Press, 1990).

The Set-Up-to-Fail Syndrome: How Good Managers Cause Great

People to Fail. Jean-François Manzoni and Jean-Louis Barsoux (Harvard Business School Press, 2002).

Orbiting the Giant Hairball: A Corporate Fool's Guide to Surviving with Grace. Gordon MacKenzie (Penguin Putnam, 1998).

1001 Ways to Reward Employees. Bob Nelson (Workman Publishing Company, 2005).

1001 Ways to Energize Employees. Bob Nelson (Workman Publishing Company, 1997).

It's All Politics: Winning in a World Where Hard Work and Talent Aren't Enough. Kathleen Kelley Reardon (Currency, 2005)

The Secret Handshake: Mastering the Politics of the Business Inner Circle. Kathleen Kelley Reardon (Currency, 2002).

The Likeability Factor: How to Boost Your L-Factor and Achieve Your Life's Dreams. Tim Sanders (Crown, 2005).

Reach for the Summit: The Definite Dozen System for Succeeding at Whatever You Do. Pat Summitt (Broadway Books, 1999).

Nurture by Nature: Understand Your Child's Personality Type—and Become a Better Parent. Paul D. Tieger and Barbara Barron-Tieger (Little, Brown, 1997).

More Than a Pink Cadillac: Mary Kay Inc.'s 9 Leadership Keys to Success. Jim Underwood (McGraw-Hill, 2003).

Articles and Guides

Gender Gaps: Where Schools Still Fail Our Children. American Association of University Women Educational Foundation (1998).

Growing Smart: What's Working for Girls in School. American Association of University Women Educational Foundation (1995).

"Women's Perceptions of the Adolescent Experience." Elaine Bell Kaplan (*Adolescence*, Fall 1997).

The following are downloadable from http://harvardbusinesson line.hbsp.harvard.edu:

"Required Reading for Executive Women—and the Companies Who Need Them." Sylvia Ann Hewlett, Carolyn Buck Luce, and Anna Fels (HBR OnPoint Collection, March 2005).

"Ways Women Lead." Judy B. Rosener (*Harvard Business Review,* November–December 1990).

"What's Holding Women Back?" Sheila Wellington, Marcia Brumit Kropf, and Paulette R. Gerkovich (*Harvard Business Review,* June 2003).

Index

About the Author

Dr. Lois P. Frankel, president of Corporate Coaching International—a Pasadena, California, consulting firm—wrote the book on coaching people to succeed in businesses large and small around the globe. Combining her experience in human resources at a *Fortune* 10 oil company with a PhD in counseling psychology from the University of Southern California, Dr. Frankel is a pioneer in the field of business coaching. For the past two decades, her unique formula has helped thousands of professionals create winning strategies to achieve superior career success and business goals. Her client list reads like a who's who of multinational corporations: Amgen, BP, McKinsey & Company, Inc., Procter & Gamble, the Walt Disney Company, and Warner Bros. are just a few of the companies that have invited her back time and again.

Sought after as a public speaker for her witty, warm, and practical presentations that actively engage the audience, Dr. Frankel is among the top international speakers featured on Better Life Media, a cable television channel in more than 425,000 hotel rooms around the globe. She is also a featured career coach on AOL.com and can be heard daily in Southern California on KNX 1070 with her coaching tip of the day. Her last two books, *Nice Girls Don't Get the Corner Office* and *Nice Girls Don't Get Rich,* are international bestsellers. For more information about Dr. Frankel, visit her Web site, www.drloisfrankel.com.

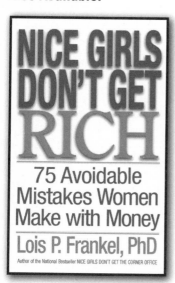